# AFRICA
## A CONTINENT REVEALED

### René Gordon

NEW
HOLLAND

This edition first published in the UK in 1992 by
New Holland (Publishers) Ltd
37 Connaught Street, London W2 2AZ

ISBN 1 85368 017 6

Design: W. Votteler
Typography: W. Reinders
Cover design: Paul Wood
Phototypeset by McManus Bros Ltd
Lithographic reproduction by Hirt & Carter Ltd
Printed and bound in Singapore by Tien Wah Press Ltd

# Photographers

T. Bannister: 198, 201, 202, 207, 208, 211, 212, 213, 214, 215, 216, 218, 219, 224, 253   R. Berger: 49, 79   D. Blum: 1, 2, 9, 12, 50, 51, 54, 85, 89, 91, 92, 93, 94, 105, 121, 122, 161, 163, 251, 252
Camerapix/M. Amin: 115, 124, 136, 137, 138, 139, 140, 141, 148, 153, 154, 155, 156, 162, 164, 165, 166, 176   G. Chesi: 29, 57, 58, 59, 60, 61, 65, 66, 67, 68, 69, 70, 71, 76, 77, 78, 98, 99, 101, 107   G. Cubitt: 126, 142, 150, 151, 158, 160, 167, 168, 175, 178, 179, 182, 191, 199, 210, 221, 223, 226, 227, 229, 232, 233, 235, 254   P. Dandliker: 56
L. Dickenson: 8   A. Elliot: 236   S. Errington: 134   Explorer/G. P. de Foy: 43, 44, 157   B. Gérard: 31, 90, 125, 127, 131   D. Goldblatt: 231, 239, 242, 243, 245, 246, 247, 248, 249, 250   H. Gruyaert: 37, 39, 40, 41, 45, 47, 48   A. Hutchinson: 30, 52, 81, 88   O. Iten: 116, 117, 118, 119, 120, 123   P. Johnson: 181, 183, 184, 185, 186, 187, 188, 189, 194, 195, 196, 197, 200, 203, 204, 205, 206, 209, 217, 220 222, 225   A. Jorgensen: 228, 244   M. Kaplan: 103, 132, 169, 170, 171, 172, 173   V. King: 38, 46, 113, 114, 147, 159, 177   G. Komnick: 238   C. Krüger: 18, 23, 24, 25, 26, 32, 35, 36, 64, 83, 95, 96, 106   Magnum/B. Barbey: 80, 82   Magnum/I. Berry: 100, 104   Magnum/Hopker: 129
Magnum/G. le Querrec: 62, 72, 73, 74   Magnum/Riboud: 42
T. McNally: 255   A. Moldvay: 128, 130   T. Nebbia: 4, 174, 193
K. Nomachi: 10, 11, 17, 19, 20, 21, 22, 53   A. Papst: 33, 34, 75
G. Philippart de Foy: 55, 86, 87, 97, 102, 108, 109, 110, 111, 112
H. Potgieter: 230, 237   Schapolawow/T. Nebbia: 6, 143, 149, 152
Schapolawow/Schliack: 144, 145, 146   K. Siebahn: 3, 5, 7
C. Stede: 13, 14, 15, 16, 133, 135   P. Steyn: 180, 190, 192
A. Sycholt: 234, 240, 241   S. Tondok: 27, 28, 63, 84

# Contents

# Consultants

**Professor Roy Siegfried** is the Director of the Percy FitzPatrick Institute of African Ornithology at the University of Cape Town. His professional career has embraced marine, freshwater and terrestrial ecology and he has carried out original research in all these fields. He has been a visiting professor in the Department of Ecology and Behavioural Biology at the University of Minnesota and a research fellow in Canada and Europe.

**Professor John Grindley** teaches Environmental Studies at the University of Cape Town. He is an ecologist with a wide range of interests and research activities including environmental problems of estuaries, coastal areas and Antarctic ecology. His professional career has involved various aspects of research and conservation as well as museum management.

He has studied and worked at several universities including Cape Town, Port Elizabeth, Southampton, Cambridge and Harvard. He has travelled widely in Africa.

# Acknowledgements

Although only one name appears on the title page, this book is the work of many people, each of whom contributed a further dimension to the whole. Just as the conductor of an orchestra brings together the gifts of individual players and brings forth sounds that are the sum of their excellence, so I have been in the fortunate position of having a number of exceptional and gifted orchestra members with me for this opus.

I have singled out those whose enthusiasm, care and intellect have left an indelible stamp on the book as it appears here; but there were many others who provided valuable support in many practical ways.

The body of the research was undertaken by Ronit Baron and Dierdre Richards who ferreted out books and papers to provide the necessary factual background to the overall thesis.

The thesis itself I owe to Professor Roy Siegfried and Professor John Grindley who originally suggested that an environmental approach to such a book was both relevant and useful. Professor Siegfried, during our valued association that goes back several years, had already instilled and encouraged in me an environmentalist point of view. Professor Grindley in his turn introduced to the book the ideas and problems that bedevil environmentalists not only in Africa, but the world over.

Sharon Anstey helped me through the early – and perhaps most difficult – part of this book when we tussled with the best ways in which to integrate ideas and the visual image. Her good taste and clear thought processes were invaluable. During the months of actual writing and research that followed, Ronit Baron organised and encouraged me, constantly analysing the work as it progressed.

In the course of the writing, many others were consulted and gave freely of their time and knowledge: Gwen Shaughnessy's excellent material on Aswan provided the background on the predicament of the Nile River; Professor John Parkington's time scale for the African continent greatly assisted in the piecing together of events; Dr Andy Smith, in his account to us of life among the Tuareg, gave tremendous insight into these desert people and their Saharan home.

For the presentation of the text and captions I am particularly indebted to Arnold Mathews who edited the book and brought to it his impeccable taste and sensitivity with words and ideas.

To all these people I owe thanks and sincerely hope that the book will in itself go some way towards giving the satisfaction that is perhaps the true reward of such endeavours.

As for any errors in the text, for these I take full responsibility; the orchestra cannot surmount the shortcomings of the conductor, nor be held accountable for her mistakes.

René Gordon, March 1980

# A new perspective

Africa accounts for a quarter of the land surface of the earth and 10 per cent of its population. Yet these statistics are too general to reveal anything of the lives, hopes and aspirations of her people. Almost half of this immense continent is either austerely arid or oppressively humid, desert or equatorial forest, both of which are hostile to man. Of the total land available, only 3 per cent can be classified as truly fertile, and a further 8 per cent as moderately so. Nor are her peoples evenly distributed over the land. In 1985 over 25 per cent of the population of the continent as a whole will be of school-going age. What will their future hold? For it is within the newly perceived limits of the land, its resources and potentials that their future lies.

For too long now the technologically advanced countries of the world have perpetuated the image of Africa as peopled by stereotypes and obscured by myth. But the time for such misconceptions is past. Wolstenholme so rightly says that Africa is still close to a fresh start – many of her mineral resources are as yet intact and many of her options are still open. These are the fundamental differences that set her apart from the global predicaments of overpopulation, pollution and the rapid depletion of non-renewable resources. However, Africa shares many of the same dilemmas and unavoidable truths that increasingly trouble this planet, and for this reason she can no longer be dealt with in isolation.

In the final analysis, Africa too is finite; her resources will not last for ever, and what is more she is running out of time. The outstanding factor that strikes a note of urgency is that Africa has one of the fastest growing populations in the world.

By the turn of the 21st century, her present numbers will have doubled, and even if birth control were strictly implemented today, tomorrow's parents have already been born. How will she feed, educate and sustain her future millions? How should she best use her vast resources for the betterment of all? How should she protect herself from a greedy world? Faced with such realities – and with the growing awareness that there is no longer time for lengthy trial and error, social experiment and profligate actions – Africa stands poised at the threshold that will determine her future.

Much of what she is now was determined by her recent past and the colonial experience. The subsequent dismissal of the African cultural heritage as inferior on one hand, and a regrettable tendency to cast aside the familiar for the new on the other, can be attributed to this

*'I think it is Africa, where man probably began, that can give men hope of a new life. By an immense combined effort Africa can save itself and give time, a vital breathing space, to the rest of the world. Man everywhere needs Africa. Even more, I believe, Africa so near to a fresh start, can set an enviable example to the older world . . .'*

*G. E. W. Wolstenholme in* Man and Africa, *1965*

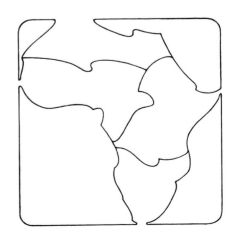

encounter between Africa and the West. African systems were overwhelmed by these technologically advanced societies who seemed, through material advantages, to offer attractive alternatives to traditional African ways. And at the time these alternatives served their exponents extremely well, for the people of the United States of America and Western Europe enjoy a material standard of living such as the world has never known before.

Nevertheless there is a growing realisation that this planet can never again support such conspicuous consumption and such ruthless exploitation of its resources. Greed and self-interest are inherently human qualities and have always had a place in our impressive arsenal of survival strategies. But we have others. Africa herself has examples that reveal that these need not be dominant. The Bushman of the Kalahari wastes and the Bedouin of the Sahara have adapted culturally so that self-control, social sanction and group interests overrule individual demands. This is not out of any altruism, but in response to their particular situations in which such patterns offer the best odds for survival. And if the immediate reply to this suggestion of alternative value systems is that these cultural adaptations are practised by people who live in the most marginal of environments, we miss the most pertinent aspect of all: the world within the next three decades will have so many people, so much pollution, be so depleted of its non-renewable resources and its renewable ones will be so degraded that ours will in fact be a marginal world.

Africa must face the fact that even if she were to share out all her wealth equally among her people, there would not be sufficient to provide each person with a standard of living comparable in any way to that of Americans or West Europeans. Indeed, on the basis of her present population growth, it is unlikely that the children being born in Africa today will even experience a standard of living as high as their parents'.

The current population problems in Africa are a direct result of fertility, mortality and migration. Until relatively recently, the African environment exercised an effective control over population. Tropical scourges such as malaria, bilharzia and river blindness were debilitating and often fatal; plague and smallpox killed off entire villages. Even in the early decades of this century, a man was considered lucky to live beyond the age of 40, and parents were resigned to losing at least some of their children through high infant mortality.

Thus, before the advent of modern medicine, the birth rate and the death rate exerted an almost equal influence on the overall population, maintaining a general equilibrium and permitting a slow and steady rate of growth. But medical technology now began to cure and control Africa's endemic diseases, pushing back the death rate. Medicine, combined initially with better nutrition and new concepts of hygiene, ensured that more children survived to maturity, thereby rapidly increasing the population.

As important as the soaring numbers has been the overwhelming – and probably irreversible – movement of peoples to the towns. Nineteenth century Europe experienced a similar phenomenon but there, for those who left the land, the industrial revolution indeed offered an attractive alternative. In Africa there were never the economic realities to meet the expectations of the new urban dweller.

Less than a hundred years ago most Africans lived on the land, sustaining themselves on what they produced. That is not to say that all practised subsistence economies, but the principle of self-sustaining systems was inherent in the traditional ways of life of the majority. Urbanisation has destroyed these systems whose advantages were never appreciated until they had already been lost. Today, the rural areas are often under-populated and desperately short of labour, for the children and elderly are left in the village while the able-bodied men turn to the towns to look for opportunities that are simply not there, and the women in turn follow their men.

Little in the history of the past century has put Africans in a position to acquire the benefits associated with industrialised economies. Throughout the continent there is a serious shortage of entrepreneurs and technological skills to build and sustain modern diversified economies. In view of widespread unemployment, the first and crucial step must be to choose the appropriate technology – or devise a new one – for the African situation: six men with ploughs and bullocks in place of a single tractor burning imported fossil fuels; roads constructed by men with picks and shovels rather than a single machine – the labour-intensive systems which can provide employment for her unskilled workers and spread the national wealth. For too long Africa has been exploited – by the colonial powers in the past, by the big powers today, and by her existing power élites – for the benefit of the relatively few.

Man's greatest gift has always been his ability to adapt to the realities of his situation. But before he can begin to cope with the problems and alternatives he must see clearly what they are. For this, education is the vital tool. The world offers most to the person who is literate. Indeed, western technology is locked in the written word and literacy has become the key to development.

There is need for compromise and for new objectives, for solutions fitted to the specific needs of Africa's people. Education for the child whose future will lie in a textile factory processing locally grown cotton, who will smelt the minerals from the African earth, who will plough the soil to feed the millions, should be geared to equipping him with the special skills he will need to best exploit Africa's unique environment. For such a child, now, abstract knowledge is largely irrelevant.

Many of the answers to Africa's problems of development, however, lie not so much in the wholesale adoption of foreign values and ideas, as in a more realistic perception of her own. Her past, her cultures and splendidly complex ecosystems may well provide exciting alternatives.

It will take patience and foresight, immense faith and impeccable judgement if people are to make the best choices; the ones most sustainable and appropriate to their needs and which will provide the greatest good for the greatest number.

As for the rest of the world, it too stands to gain much from the African experience. And it is in the belief that from an understanding of the environment can come the harmony and equilibrium which still eludes the rest of the world that this book was written. It was the motivation behind the choice of photographs, the material for the captions and the ideas represented in the text. Visually we have chosen to portray the Africa of splendid and varied landscapes little touched by the hand of man; of people whose way of life is still closely linked to the earth; of her intricate ecosystems of such essential and humbling beauty that all human endeavour retreats into a wider perspective. But if the visual image is romantic and nostalgic, the text and captions are committed to the realities and the future.

# North Africa

The Sahara dominates North Africa like a sea of arid land: some dare cross it but most cling to its margins as fishermen to the shore. This spreading expanse of windblown grit and sere gravel plains, of pale orange dunes and massifs of desolate sandstone is, in all its guises, hostile to man. For thousands of years he has hunted and traded, herded livestock and raided his neighbours around its edges.

Only the Tuareg and the Bedouin are at ease deep in the desert, for through long association, they have come to know it as their home, to understand its changing moods and accept its frugal offerings.

Not only is the Sahara desert by definition entirely arid, but it is also a region of trying climatic extremes. Temperatures can soar beyond 40 °C day after brutal day, but the night time temperatures regularly plunge to 0 °C and frost is a common phenomenon. For several months of the year conditions are made even worse by the parching *Hamadas* winds from the north east that mercilessly drive sand across the wastes.

This is a world of camels and fatalists, and to this day relatively few penetrate its inner emptinesses. Some live close to the oases which scatter the desert, growing dates and, where irrigation allows, barley and vegetables; others still lead long lines of camels heavily laden with salt and cloth and Western-made goods along ancient caravan routes that have seen trade across the Sahara for more than a thousand years. But the majority of North Africa's peoples live along the Sahara's margins: the Nile Valley, the narrow strip of land abutting the Mediterranean in the north, and the region dominated by the tall, snow-capped peaks of the Atlas Mountains.

Sahara means deserts, not one but many, and it is likely that there has been a Sahara since prehistoric times, yet it has not always been the size it is today or been situated exactly where it is now. Researchers have found strong evidence that relates the story of this, the largest desert in the world, to the major fluctuations in earth climate over many many millions of years. The desert sands are themselves estimated to be at least 60 million years old.

The close relationship between the North African desert zone and climatic changes elsewhere in the world was clearly illustrated during the most recent Ice Ages when the polar ice caps expanded over far greater areas of the earth than they do now. And with their successive advances and retreats, so North Africa's desert zone was vitally

*'If the present growth trends in world population, industrialisation, pollution, food production and resource depletion continue unchanged, the limits to growth on this planet will be reached some time within the next one hundred years.'*

The Limits to Growth *1972*

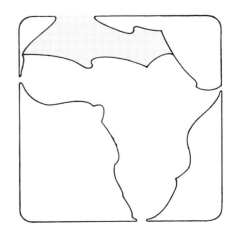

affected, for not only did the Sahara shrink and expand in concert with the changes at the northern and southern extremities of the globe, but its position moved too. At one time, before sea water engulfed the Mediterranean, desert winds howled over the areas that later became Italy's tuna fishing grounds.

However, the desert zone has generally occupied the northern regions of Africa and this accounts to some extent for the popular view of the Sahara as an impenetrable barrier between the North African coastal regions and the rest of Africa to the south. Yet the northern and southern margins of the Sahara are undeniably different from one another and scientists normally regard the regions to the north in similar light to Europe, and consider Africa proper to lie south of the desert. For instance, the trees of Africa's Mediterranean littoral are essentially those of Europe – pine and oak, olive and cedar, while to the south grow acacias and hardy scrub, euphorbias and resilient grasses.

So vast is the Sahara that its northern and southern margins belong to entirely different ecological zones. In the south the desert gradually merges into the sub-tropical regions characterised by sporadic but violent summer downpours and a cool dry season. The northern margins, on the other hand, are part of the Mediterranean zone with its winter rains and hot, drought-stricken summers. It is therefore not unnatural that the plants adapted to sub-Saharan Africa should find the Mediterranean coast a hostile environment, and vice versa.

The changes in the Sahara over the past 10 000 years have been the subject of much study and, in terms of early man, research has centred on two areas he is known to have occupied: the highlands of what is today the central Sahara desert, and the Nile Valley.

Much of the Sahara desert is monotonously flat, gravel-strewn rather than blanketed with sand, and in its midst two highland massifs dominate the surrounding landscape: the Tibesti Mountains and the Tassili n'Ajjer. Scientists have found relics that not only prove that man once lived here but that also document his development from a simple neolithic existence as a hunter-gatherer to that of a cattle herder. But as a chronicle of Saharan man, nothing they have found can equal the magnificent rock engravings and paintings of these regions.

About 6 000 years ago this was another world. Man the hunter pursued oryx and giraffe over broad savannahs and flocks of birds dipped low over shimmering grassland.

In the Tassili and Tibesti highlands man took up residence in the shelter of the rocks and pursued the great herds of antelope that made gratifyingly easy targets on the open plains. And in the superb engravings and paintings he then made he celebrated the satisfaction of the hunt and the munificence of nature.

Today the desert winds whisper and growl among the deserted rock shelters. The occasional Tuareg still passes this way and for a moment the human voice breaks the desert silences, but only briefly, for this is no longer a place for man.

There is no water and it is all but impossible to imagine that these stark mountains were once shaded by juniper and oak. But the record of man's occupancy is irrefutably there, preserved from the merciless sun in the shadows of overhanging rocks.

The most ancient work discovered here so far is an engraving of an elephant picked out in profile against the mother rock. Later works portray oryx and ostrich, hippopotamus and crocodile – none of which could survive here now.

Yet this was but an interlude in the total history of the Sahara. About 4 000 years ago the most recent swing towards a dry era had begun. The desert started to grow once more and as it became more dominant, so its changes were reflected in the lives of the Saharan rock artists. The desert asserted itself, albeit extremely slowly, and the trees thinned and the grasses became poorer. However, at this point in time, man had improved his survival strategies and was no longer entirely dependent on nature's bounty. He had become a herder of cattle. Therefore the altering grasslands did not disturb his equilibrium for they made fine pasture and his cattle grew sleek and fat. For the moment, man in the Sahara enjoyed a sense of well-being and this coincides with the high point in his artistic expression. He recorded his life with an exuberant confidence that is splendidly expressed in fluidly representational style; his cattle are carefully drawn and executed in vivid polychrome.

But the desertification process was inexorable and just as the rock artists portrayed the times of plenty, so they recorded the gradual yet growing

hostility of their environment. Did the birdsong gradually fade as years of drought came to outnumber the years of rain? Did the heavens bestow sporadic showers where earlier they had drenched the earth? We shall probably never know.

By some 2 500 years ago the pastoralists had deserted the Tassili and Tibesti highlands. And in their rock art of this period, there is a corresponding decline in sensitivity and care. In the works that follow, warriors are depicted and, later still, the camel makes its appearance, marking the end of the era of plenty in this part of Africa.

Pastoralism has never afforded men the surpluses – and the security – enjoyed by the cultivator whose efforts are rewarded by bulging granaries and an absence of want.

The concept of sowing and reaping crops – cereals in particular – is believed to have come from Mesopotamia's fertile river valleys. It was a way of life that transplanted with natural ease to Africa's Nile Valley, for the environment closely matched that of the land between the Tigris and Euphrates, and moreover this part of Africa had long been a crossroads of ideas. No matter how hostile the Sahara, man and animals had always been able to travel along its margins, and more especially north and south along the Nile.

No one knows exactly when man first planted seeds into the rich mud left by the receding Nile floods, but archaeologists working near Aswan in Egypt have found grains of cultivated barley that have been firmly dated as from between 17 000 and 18 000 years ago.

Cultivation of the Nile flood plain proved to be rewarding for it is abundantly fertile and the natural advantages it offers Egyptians today must have been even more apparent then. The Nile's special gift is its annual flood that bestows a layer of nutrient-rich silt over the land.

The river rises in the high mountains that border the East African Rift Valley and courses more than 6 500 kilometres northwards along a natural trough in the land surface before fanning out in a generous delta where it empties into the Mediterranean.

Much of its productiveness derives from the luxuriant papyrus beds of the Nile Sudd in its upper course. Here the river spreads over the land creating a vast swamp overgrown with reeds and infested with mosquitoes. Beyond the Sudd, the Nile is joined by several tributaries, largest of which is the Blue Nile turgid with topsoil scoured from the Ethiopian highlands.

The Nile is a world within itself, an ecosystem evolved over many thousands of years and insulated from the rest of Africa by the desert that hugs close to both its banks. In this area, man has depended entirely on the river system for his survival and out of its fertility came the stability in which the great kingdoms flourished. The Pharaohs must have fully recognised how closely their power was linked to the Nile, for its annual flood ensured the crops that fed the people and thus maintained the peace. The kings in return acknowledged the river's beneficence by deifying it in the person of Hapi, the river god.

So the relationship between the Egyptians and the river developed, and the people learnt to exploit it to greater effect; to irrigate the fields, opening up more and more land to crops. They built barrages to help hold back the flood waters and they led the silt-laden flood waters to enclosed fields so that their usefulness and nutrients could be extended over a larger area.

Out of the surpluses the great river produced, came the leisure to pursue crafts and improve technology, while its plenty sustained a steadily growing population even though there were years when the flood failed and brought famine, and others when it swept all away before it.

As their wealth grew and their tastes became more refined, the rulers of the Nile looked beyond the confines of their valley for more resources to satisfy their increasingly sophisticated wants. While the peasants were content to work the land that provided them with the staples, the Pharaohs and the nobles desired luxuries from further afield: cedarwood from Lebanon and gold from the Nubian hills.

The Nile Valley no longer could sustain their ambitions and their lifestyles. They needed slaves to build their grandiose monuments, timber for their couches, ivory and precious metals to adorn their palaces and their persons: and, looking to the African hinterland to fulfil these desires, they first exploited the land southward along the Nile and then, later, with domestication of the camel, across to West Africa. The historian Basil Davidson in *The Africans: An Entry to Cultural History* describes how 'a travel-wearied merchant of Alexandria relaxes in his bath one Friday afternoon towards the year 1100 and then, before sitting down to dinner, scribbles a note to a partner in Cairo.

"I have just arrived from Almeria in Spain. Your business friend in Moroccan Fez sent me there a bar of gold – certainly from the Sudan – so as to buy Spanish silk for you. I thought this not a good idea, however, and am sending you the gold instead. At the same time a friend of your business friend delivered me a certain quantity of ambergris which I also forward herewith. He wants you to send back five flasks of musk of the same value. Please sell the ambergris when you get this letter and buy the musk, because I have to send it off at once."' This was Egypt's golden age.

But theirs was not the only civilization of that time bent on imperial might and exploitation. Across the Mediterranean the Romans were also on the ascendant, looking for more food, more slaves, more power. In retrospect it is not surprising that these two civilizations would clash in pursuit of similar interests.

Rome brought to an end Egyptian dynastic rule and took for herself the riches of the Nile Valley. Rome alone, however, does not account for Egypt's subsequent decline; it was also due to the limits of the Nile itself. Neither the Roman nor Egyptian rulers were aware that the growing populations of the Nile Valley were posing a threat that would in time tax the environment to the point where Egyptians came to taste increasingly, poverty, shortage of food and lowered expectations. Their defeat at the hand of Rome was nothing compared to their defeat at the hand of nature.

Realisation of the dangers of overpopulation has come only recently to Egypt – and to the world at large. In the 1940s planners still lent their energies to coaxing more from the river rather than controlling Egypt's soaring numbers. Since the Second World War her population growth rate has been a staggering 2,3 per cent and in the Nile Valley population density averages 90 people to the square kilometre. Cairo alone has a population of almost 4 500 000 and is growing larger year by year as the effects of rural poverty drive people to the cities.

There are no easy solutions, nor can the Nile provide any additional answers; it is already at its limit of productivity, and ambitious plans to extend these limits further, have failed. Perhaps

greatest proof of this is the Aswan project which was intended to provide food for Egypt's future millions. Yet the real problem of bringing down the birth rate escaped attention until the realities of the situation could no longer be avoided. Aswan's much vaunted answers have proved both costly and inadequate.

Over-exploitation has also been a dominant theme along the North African coastal regions. Here the productive land is confined between the Sahara and the Mediterranean. At its widest it is a strip 300 kilometres broad along the coast and it dwindles to a mere ribbon of green in several places. Yet in Roman times this area was considered so fertile that it became the main source of food for the empire.

The Romans were not the first to settle here; long before, relatives of the Berbers of the Atlas Mountains terraced the hillsides and grazed their herds over the land, always careful to retain its usefulness. Their numbers were relatively sparse and therefore land was conversely plentiful and their long occupation had little detrimental impact on the environment.

The Romans were, however, not seeking a subsistence level of production. They needed grain and olive oil, vines and fruit trees in abundance and they had the technology to coax the maximum from the soil. They built graceful aqueducts to carry water for irrigation and developed sophisticated terracing and drainage systems, adding to the earlier terraces constructed by the Berber peasants.

For almost three hundred years North Africa was the grain basket of the Roman Empire. It was acknowledged at the time that there were huge profits to be made there, and an appointment to the North African provinces was certain to make a man wealthy.

The appetite of the Romans knew no bounds. To meet their constant demands for more food from North Africa they began to till the marginal areas on the slopes of hills and the edges of the desert. In their hunger for fresh land they even felled the forests which had covered as much as half of the North African littoral. When Rome fell and withdrew her influence from this foreign soil, the Berber peasants remained on the land where they continued to farm on a modest scale.

In the 7th century the tenure of the land was

disputed once more when Arab invaders galloped westwards along the littoral. They came carrying the banner of Islam, but theirs was not simply a religious foray. They also wanted fresh pasture for their sheep, goats and camels. Pushed westwards by this invasion, the Berbers retreated, some to the region of the Atlas Mountains, others to the Saharan wastes.

Successive ownership of the North African littoral now began to reveal its toll. The Arabs were not farmers, but nomads and warriors unconcerned with good husbandry and the dangers of erosion. Their priority was grazing. Where the Romans had cleared the forest to plant crops, the Arabs now brought in their sheep and goats which stripped the last vestige of plant cover from the soil. The forces of erosion – wind and water – were free to devastate the land.

The Roman appetite for great and bloody spectacle also had a disastrous effect on North Africa's wildlife. Their requirements were such that today not a single lion still hunts these areas, which once also had been home to creatures such as ostrich, antelope and cheetah. These animals were pursued to their last and shipped, live to Italy to be killed as part of the 'bread and circuses' provided by their masters for the amusement of the populace.

Today much of this once fertile area is a wasteland, unproductive and barren. Furthermore the recovery of this abused earth is painfully slow now that erosion has played its part unchallenged for so long.

The Berbers found their new home scarcely more generous than their old. They settled in the foothills of the Atlas Mountains and cultivated the land along the coast. And although many of their traditional farming methods are not essentially destructive, the increasing demand for food within a very limited supply of land has placed intolerable stresses on the environment. Too poor to afford the fertilizers, pesticides and modern technology that would increase yields, the farmers look instead for more land to cultivate on the slopes. Moreover, as each family has grown, so the inherited land has had to be shared between more and more people; fields have become smaller as they have been divided time and again from generation to generation so that not only are they no longer an economically viable size but they are also widely scattered. The energy wasted in working these little plots is counterproductive and the entire land tenure system inhibits any technological advance.

While the Berbers of the Atlas Mountains have found their livelihood increasingly unrewarding, their desert cousins the Tuareg still enjoy a rare freedom. These steely-eyed warriors, closely veiled in indigo cloth, move about the desert margins with their herds. Traditionally they have controlled the caravan routes of the Sahara, levying duties on all goods, but the era of trans-Saharan trade is waning and governments levy the monies that the Tuareg still consider their rightful due.

Like the Berbers they have adopted the Islamic faith and many of their raids on neighbouring peoples in search of slaves and camels have been undertaken in the name of Allah.

By generally marrying only among their own they have also kept the distinctive Caucasian features of their race. Their singular identity is further maintained by the ethic in which a man's honour is his proudest virtue and his hospitality his guarantee of survival.

Although the Tuareg nobles claim that any form of manual labour is below them, their survival thus far is a tribute to their skills as camel herders. While their slaves generally remain at desert oases and grow crops which the aristocracy tax in kind, the Tuareg themselves pursue the life they love best; that of warrior-nomads. In their annual migration they reveal a remarkable empathy with their desert home, reaping its wild grasses to make flour, and gathering wild plants to augment their largely milk-based diet. But their wise use of the desert is most evident in the manner in which they pasture their camels and goats, for to survive they have had to recognise the limits of their environment. They well know that to overgraze the meagre pastures will mean that they cannot return there for many years: and given the marginal nature of this habitat such profligate behaviour would surely mean their doom.

The equilibrium enjoyed by the Tuareg in the Sahara is denied most of North Africa's other peoples, for this is not an intrinsically productive and wealthy part of this world. The current rise in petroleum prices underscores the reality that Libya and Algeria will not be able to depend on their oil supplies for ever. Morocco and Egypt's phosphate wealth will probably be exhausted within the next 60 years and there do not appear to be many other resources still awaiting discovery in the Sahara. Even dreams of making the desert bloom under extensive irrigation are unrealistic in terms of the foreseeable future.

Water is not the only limiting factor; the soils are generally infertile and would require huge inputs of costly fertilisers because the winds that have for thousands of years whipped across the desert have carried away the precious topsoil, leaving an impoverished and fragile surface.

Only nature herself could ever bring a flush of green back to the Sahara and this may happen one day far from now. Scientists already speak of the onset of a new Ice Age and just as the great climatic changes of the past revitalised rivers which flowed through the now arid watercourses and emptied into shallow lakes filled with fish, so it iş possible that similar forces may come into play again.

But the people of North Africa face imminent problems that will not wait for some fortuitous change in nature's favours. Already they are dangerously close to exhausting their resources – minerals, land and water. Furthermore the burden of rampant population growth has severely curtailed developments that might ensure a better future: diversification of the economies, the education of people in technical skills, and self-sufficiency in food.

In each country the alternatives are becoming unavoidably apparent: the national wealth can either continue to be spread unevenly and thinly over the growing population or be distributed to bring greater benefit to all.

Poverty and ignorance have delayed any meaningful reduction in the birth rate. Many North Africans still believe that a large family is an insurance against disaster, and until education and responsible government action awakens them to the true effects of an uncontrolled birth rate, the future is indeed bleak.

**1** At the approach of dusk these statues at Luxor reflect the fading light of Ra, Sun God of ancient Egypt.

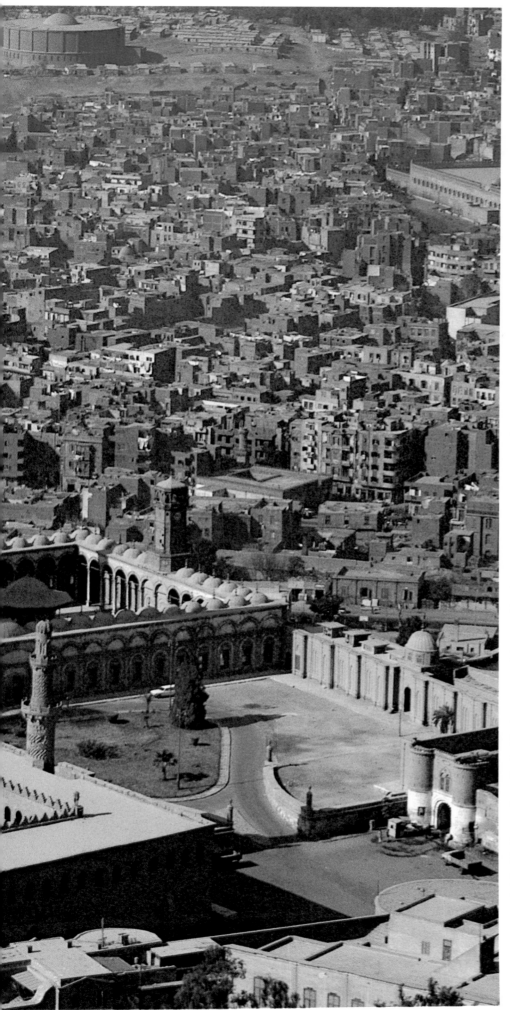

**2** Cairo's mosque stands apart from the city's hubbub. For more than a thousand years, Islam has ordered the spiritual life of most of Egypt's people, but it is the Nile that has sustained them since time immemorial. For Egypt is a desert land, and the Nile its major source of life. Every year between June and September the river comes down in flood and lavishes fresh soil on the flatlands and delta. From this rich tilth come crops, crops so abundant that they have nurtured Egypt's ever-increasing numbers.

For the Pharaohs there must have been a deep sense of security in the river's annual cycle. They well knew that their power depended as much on grain as on gold, and that the harvests were linked inevitably with the river. But the Nile was not always benevolent. In years when the floods failed there was famine; when the river raged wild, it brought hunger and death.

Wise men pondered its vagaries, seeking to understand this force that determined so much of their lives and, in understanding, to control it and make it ever more productive.

And the Egyptians succeeded – methods improved and crops became ever more plentiful. Yet in their essential dependence on the flood, there was little difference between the cultivator of predynastic times who planted his crops directly into the mud of the receding floodwaters, and the fellah at the turn of the present century. Later generations had developed basin irrigation which allowed the cultivation of areas not normally reached by the flood, and in relatively modern times, barrages across the Nile have helped hold back the floodwaters and extend the growing season. Hand-operated *shadoofs* still slop water bag by bag into channels to irrigate the cotton, the dates, the apricot trees.

As long as the river replenished the natural elements removed by man, the system sustained itself. Indeed, it embodied the very harmony for which the Egyptians strove in their architecture, their religious beliefs, their way of life. But over the millennia, no-one sensed the sinister disharmony that would emerge with a mad momentum of its own. Between 1800 and 1950 the population of the Nile valley increased tenfold, and only recently did forward-thinking men begin to perceive that even as benevolent a lifespring as the Nile has limits, and that these limits have been reached.

**3** Commerce spills out onto Cairo streets crammed with people. There are 39 000 000 people in Egypt now – and half are under 20. How will Egypt educate, feed and gainfully employ them?

3

4  6

5

**4** A TV set and camel make this Cairene a man of means – but in his own eyes, his prosperity and future also lie in his children.

**5** Part of the vibrant street life of Cairo.

**6** The Romans would not allow camels within their city walls because the vile smell frightened the horses and offended the people. In Egypt the camel is still too valuable a beast for such discrimination, and the camel market in Cairo does brisk business.

7

8

**7** A sandstorm lashes the Nile delta and as a fellah hurries home, egrets hunch against the gritty onslaught.

**8** Irrigation channels etch precise patterns in a Nile landscape as ancient as the Pharaohs. Over the centuries, along its 6 500 kilometres, the river had been dammed and barraged, channelled and slowed, and yet man could never disturb its essential tempo. Then, in 1971, the once eternal rhythms changed forever. Just above Aswan, dwarfing all previous attempts to harness the river, the High Dam was built. Conceived in the 1940s, this grand scheme was hailed as the solution to Egypt's most pressing problems, and as a bold undertaking that would carry the country into the 21st century.

Today's figures reveal its many failures, largely because the planners accepted population growth as an irresistible force, and directed their energies towards feeding and employing future millions, rather than controlling their numbers. By the time the four-kilometre dam wall was completed, the population had grown by 30% and had reached levels forecast for the year 2000 . . . the 12% gain in arable land was already inadequate.

The High Dam is handicapped by costly imperfections; some were anticipated, others not. In the original masterplan, phosphate fertilizers were to compensate the loss of flood-borne silt to the farmlands below the wall. But 40 years ago fertilizers were cheap and no-one could foresee that phosphates, like oil, would become prohibitively expensive.

As intended, the lake does provide Egypt with more arable land – though only half the area originally expected – and perennial irrigation permits two, even three, harvests a year. But in the very ditches that lead water to the new fields, the bilharzia snail flourishes as never before. Eight out of ten people working this land suffer the debilitating disease it carries and here a man is lucky if he feels well enough to work three hours a day – or reaches the age of 30. There is a cure, both costly and difficult to administer to the peasants, and copper sulphate introduced to the water to kill off the snails is expensive.

While the High Dam spares the most populous areas of Egypt the angry moods of the river, the fishermen along the coast have come to realise that Hapi, god of the Nile, controlled their fortunes too. Suddenly their sardine catches fell by 95% and the Italians far across the Mediterranean found their tuna nets empty for the Nile no longer washed nutrients into the sea to sustain the sardines on which the tuna fed. Such was the influence of the Nile; but who can account for the intricacy of a system built up over thousands of years?

The Aswan scheme does not entirely sever the river from its delta, but today the waters come down in a controlled, much-diminished flow. Without the flood to add tons of silt to the fertile delta, sea currents have begun to eat away at the land, and without the rush of sweet water to keep the sea at bay, salty water has begun to percolate upstream, contaminating the soil which for centuries provided Egypt with its most lavish harvests. Salt also promises to destroy the area under perennial irrigation, for the high evaporation rate leaves a sterile layer of salt on once productive land. To remedy this, wells and drainage systems must be built, and electric pumps installed – at a monumental cost equal to that of the dam itself.

The High Dam experiment has not realised the dreams of its promotors but it would be wrong to see the project in entirely negative terms: below the dam navigation is easier, Lake Nasser may yet provide a freshwater fishery and, as a result of the scheme, Egypt enjoys an almost embarrassing excess of hydro-electric power for a country just reaching the industrial age. But what in reality has Egypt gained? Given the credits and the debits, not very much.

*Following page* (9): Beyond a narrow strip on either bank, the desert hugs the Nile.

**10, 11, 12** Head swathed in the traditional *tagilmust* of more than six metres of indigo cloth, a man of the central Sahara scans the desert (10). His ancestors knew its closest secrets, but only when they domesticated the camel could they trade across its wastes.

The camel originated in North America, crossed the ancient land bridge at the Bering Straits and, on its long westward journey across the thirstlands of Asia, evolved and adapted to the desert environment. It is singularly suited to a life where food and water are sporadic. In the desperate heat of a North African summer, it can go without food or water for seven days, losing up to a quarter of its body mass without ill-effect. But when it finally reaches water, the camel can gulp 120 litres in 10 minutes. This astounding quantity passes directly into the tissues, not the blood, eliminating the shock to the system that would kill any other animal exposed to such dehydration.

The dromedary or one-humped camel – the only type seen in North Africa – is best appreciated through the eyes of a cameleer. He endures the camel's poor humour, is patient at its unwillingness to learn, and shows forbearance at its slowness to breed; but its strength, its immense endurance and its nutritious milk atone for such minor imperfections. Its broad feet carry it over hot dunes (11) or jagged plains with equal ease. When the winds drive stinging sand (following page: 12), the camel's long lashes shield its eyes, its nostrils pinch shut. Even the hardiest and least palatable desert plant is a source of food. Thus, it is not surprising that man in Africa has seen fit to tolerate this surly, foul-smelling but indispensable beast.

10
11

**13, 14, 15, 16** For all its lack of social graces, the camel is central to the long and fascinating story of caravan trade across the Sahara. Long lines of them (13) still move heavily laden, along the ancient routes. The unwieldy cargoes piled upon their backs reflect changing times and changing values, but one commodity has remained of unusual value to the people of West Africa: salt.

The phenomenon is party explained by the environment of Africa's tropical west coast where the heavy rains have continually leached much of the salt from the soil. Not only do its peoples feel the need for more, but the plants and creatures, all of which require sodium chloride for their well-being, compete for what little there is.

So imported salt has long been a highly prized item of trade among West Africans. What is more, many of them maintain that only rock salt is 'real' salt which traditionally comes from Bilma and Taoudenné in the central Sahara.

It is said that a man who works the salt mines of Bilma never returns, and that a man who risks the desert to buy it takes his life in his hands. But profit makes a man brave and to this day the salt caravans make the perilous three months' journey.

Tough and opportunistic, the Tuareg and Tubu (14) have a long association with this trade. They lead their camels along routes neither well marked nor blessed with frequent waterholes (15). A single convoy may number a thousand camels, some to carry provisions over this cruelly barren part of

the desert, others to provide milk. Some will perish along the way, but those that do return are laden with heavy rectangular slabs of salt hewn and moulded by the salt miners of the desert.

At the riverside markets of the Niger and Lake Chad, the caravaneers turn an excellent profit and find no shortage of keen buyers. Hacked from the slabs and crudely crushed, it is weighed out (16) like a precious metal, and there was a time, long ago, when it fetched its weight in gold.

*Following page* (17): Dates and dwellings at Timimoun, one of the oases that relieves the desolate emptiness of the Sahara.

15

16

**18** The nomadic Tuareg know many such waterholes hidden between rocks or below desert precipices.

**19** Islam and Allah – and a basic fatalism – fortify men in the desert.

**20** Small glasses and a tiny pot of sweet strong tea welcome the traveller. There are greetings and the polite exchange of news. How is your family? Has Allah made your journey an easy one?

The first tiny glassful goes to the honoured guest. Then the men are served in order of status and soon the pot is empty, refilled and emptied again. Good manners require each man to drink three glasses of the steaming, acrid-sweet tea which is savoured with the appreciation that Westerners accord to fine wines. Much later the sugar-drenched leaves will be relished by the children.

This ritual is no haphazard cultural development: the offering and the taking of refreshment between these men who share the desert is the outward sign of a pact of friendship that can at any time be called upon to provide mutual help.

Beyond this commitment to help lie safeguards to survival, nowhere more apparent than at the waterhole where the desert code ensures each man his share and no more. Such a society cannot afford a greed or indulgence which might lead to conflict and thus further endanger its already precarious existence.

**21** Palms swish and bend as the desert wind casts a haze of sand over the oasis of Kerzaz.

*Following page* (22): South of the desolate Hoggar Mountains lies 'the garden of Hell' . . . sandblasted expanses of dunes and rocky plains so daunting that even the Tuareg will not venture there. But the Sahara has not always been a desert. Early man hunted oryx and giraffe over these very plains, and elephant and hippo disturbed its shallow lakes. The drying-out process was gradual and only recently was it clearly understood, for it relates directly to the alternating shrinkage and expansion of the polar ice caps during the most recent Ice Ages. Conceivably, these same forces may in the distant future restore the Sahara to its former fruitfulness.

24

25

**23, 24** In the oppressive silences of the Tassili 'n Ajjer it is difficult to conceive that here, in the middle of the world's largest desert, there was once bird song and women's laughter. Yet engraved and painted on countless rockfaces by unknown men is a record of an age when the Sahara was home to the herder and huntsman and creatures of the African savannah.

The work of these rock artists creates a singular chronicle of Saharan prehistory, for the paintings and engravings go back some 8 000 years during which the people of the Tassili 'n Ajjer experienced the gradual change of their environment from a juniper-scented land of plenty to the desert as we know it today.

Stylistically this prehistoric art falls into various fairly distinct periods of which, without doubt, the finest was that of the pastoralists between 5 000 and 6 000 years ago. Although – as we now know – the drying out of the Sahara was well under way, the herdsmen saw their cattle grow sleek and fat (24) and the hunter (23) found easy quarry as woodland gave way to open grassland, and he celebrated his satisfaction in rock paintings which are among the most vivid and compelling expressions of prehistoric man anywhere. But the desiccation progressed inexorably and as the tall grassland gave way to steppe, so the paintings of cattle become fewer and smaller and the change of the environment is paralleled by a decadence in the art. Later influences and events recorded on the sandstone are of historical rather than artistic significance. They show contact with the Egyptians, chariot-borne invaders and the introduction of the camel; but there is little of the earlier attention to detail or sense of spontaneity.

Gradually the people withdrew to the margins of the desert, and for 4 000 years the Tassili 'n Ajjer was visited only by passing Tuareg. It was not until 1909 that its secrets were revealed to the world.

**25** These paintings have been preserved in the shadows of the overhanging rock and, paradoxically, by the same process of desiccation that finally drove the rock artists from the Tassili 'n Ajjer.

39

**26** A fruit vendor dozes under the intense North African sun.

**27** In Ghardaia, Algeria, a network of narrow streets leads to the mosque on the hill. The simplicity of the minaret is carried through to the stark interior of the mosque, in keeping with the asceticism of the Muslims who inhabit this part of North Africa.

**28** Cascades of white, blue and ochre houses reach from the flurry of Ghardaia's marketplace to its distant minaret.

**27 28**

40

**29, 30** A cellar on the island of Djerba off the Tunisian coast (29) and these ruins at Dejmila in Algeria (30) bear testimony to the Roman occupation of the North African Maghreb.

Imperial Rome was the first foreign exploiter of Africa. Over three centuries, her insatiable desire for grand and bloody spectacle left this entire region destitute of wild animals such as lion and elephant. In a single day, at the opening of the Colosseum, 5 000 creatures were put to death. Yet, for the Romans, the Maghreb was a source of food as well as of circus delights. With exploitation they brought innovation and soon their methods had transformed the land into a cornucopia of vines, olives and grain. As Rome's demand for food grew, so cultivation was pushed to its limits, setting in motion the forces of erosion which – after later Arab neglect of the fields – left much of the Maghreb a wasteland.

**31** With good soil at a premium, dates and olives occupy the best land while the village holds tenuously to barren valley walls.

29

30  31

**32** With concentration and care, a Koranic scholar transcribes passages onto a wooden tablet at an Islamic school in southern Libya. Islam was brought to Africa by the Arabs in the 7th century and it spread quickly to West Africa where it remains a powerful force. Its success in this area has been the subject of much discussion, but without doubt Islamic schooling offered an attractive entrée to trade and commerce, similar to the way in which Eton and Harrow opened the doors to power for Englishmen in the past.

**33** As sunlight dips into her home, a cave-dweller of the Matmata Mountains in Tunisia spins wool on a primitive spindle. The quest for security probably accounts for these dwellings carved out of sandstone, but the superb insulation must have been as important in the desert climate where the deadening heat of the day is followed by the bitter cold of night. About 700 such homes exist, the rooms excavated off central air-wells which also serve as courtyards.

**34** Open workshops are typical of North Africa. Here, at Djerba, a craftsman deftly weaves blankets of wool, camel and goat hair. Simple double-bed looms like this are also used for making the exquisite carpets beloved of the desert nomads and eagerly sought after by discerning Westerners.

32 33
34

**35** These buildings at Rhat in Libya reveal how beautifully form follows function in the vernacular architecture of North Africa, where a maze of buildings forms a remarkably effective defence against the relentless desert climate. Step out of the sunlight, through one of the small doorways and the cool darkness is a relief. This dimness is a necessary compromise for bigger windows would allow warmth to escape during the chill of the desert night, heat to pour in during the day, and sandstorms to invade the home.

Buildings huddle close onto narrow streets and the interlocking angles of thick mud walls cast welcome shadows. Mud is the obvious building material: readily available and easily worked into air-dried bricks, it provides fine insulation. Wood, on the other hand, is scarce and the flat roofs are therefore suspended with mini-

mum structural support across narrow rooms. Since rain hardly falls, drainage is not a problem – hence the flat roofs so typical of North African architecture.

**36** Granaries at Médenine, Tunisia, where wheat, barley and dates are stored.

*Following page* (37): Imilchil seems one with the earth as early morning light tints village and mountains the same muted colours. Every year, here in the Atlas Mountains, thousands of Berbers meet for the famous gathering of their people. A few months before the event, the marriageable girls in each family are force-fed a diet rich in cream to make them plumply desirable. For, at Imilchil, the serious task of arranging marriages takes place, fathers negotiating matches that serve family interests.

35  36

**38** It takes two camels to drive this wooden plough through the hard, red earth where wheat will be sewn.

**39** As girls dawdle along the footpath, a Berber leads his cow to Imilchil market. The patchwork of tiny fields typifies parts of the world where land is divided and redivided as it is passed from generation to generation. In the High Atlas, as elsewhere, this is counter-productive; such fields are often small and widely dispersed and neither economically viable nor likely to permit innovative farming. The Berbers cling to this uneconomic system and once the immediately available land has been allocated to the growing family, fields are laid out on unsuitable land on the slopes. Erosion is the companion of poor land use everywhere in Africa and here in the High Atlas the already niggardly topsoil is disappearing at an alarming rate.

**40** As summer draws to an end in the High Atlas, the harvest is brought in from the valleys and foothills. Whole villages turn out to help with the threshing, in dusty scenes reminiscent of biblical times. On the specially prepared terrace, donkeys plod round and round, their hooves separating the grain from the straw.

**41** A study in chiaroscuro at Imilchil sheep market where business suits (centre left) mingle incongruously with the animated Berbers and their pungent sheep.

*Following page* (42): Their steely impassive faces mirror the harsh realities of their desert world.

**43** Indigo cloth and rich adornments contrast exquisitely with the translucently pale complexion of this Berber girl, her eyes modestly downcast. The origins of her people are uncertain for they are distinctly Caucasian as opposed to the semitic Arabs of North Africa and the negroid peoples further south. However, there is no doubt that her ancestors commanded North Africa's Mediterranean littoral long before the Arab invasion. Then, either to escape the Arabs or because of population pressure, some of the Berbers took to the desert where they became the warrior nomads known as the Tuareg, while others became settled in the area dominated by the icy peaks of the Atlas Mountains.

**44** The brilliance of her eyes equalling the splendour of her dress, a Berber woman at a wedding feast.

43  44  45

**45** Dye vats like these at Fez have been in use since Roman times when Moroccan leather was already much esteemed. Just as it dazzles the eye, so the tannery affronts the nostril, for the skins are not fully cleaned before being soaked in the dye. The dyeing completed, the leather is loaded onto donkeys and taken a good distance from the city to be dried.

**46** Dazzling skeins of wool hang out to dry in the maze of narrow lanes in the dyers' *souk* in the *medina,* or old city, of Marrakesh. A traditionally camera-shy Moroccan woman hides her face as she scurries along in her enveloping *djellaba.*

**47, 48** Wool dyers in the *medina* of Fez.

*Following page* (49): A frenzy of hooves and gunfire greets King Hassan II of Morocco at a celebration in his honour at Marrakesh.

**50** It is quite possible that 4 000 years ago women in the Sahara and on its fringes pounded wild grains just as these Tuareg are doing here. Rain rarely falls in the desert but when it does, ephemeral grasses sweep softly over the land, providing a harvest for these people.

**51** Desert nomads and their donkeys pick their way over a shattered landscape.

**52** In the shelter of her tent, a Tuareg woman of low caste makes leather scabbards for trade.

**53** Since dark goats have greater endurance than white varieties in the desert, Tuareg tend to breed the darker shades and this preference is mirrored in the colour of their homespun cloaks. Surprisingly, tests have shown that dark cloaks are no less effective against desert heat than light ones. Worn loose over other clothing, the dark cloth appears to encourage cooling convection currents beneath the garment, offsetting the extra radiation absorbed by the dark surface.

52  53

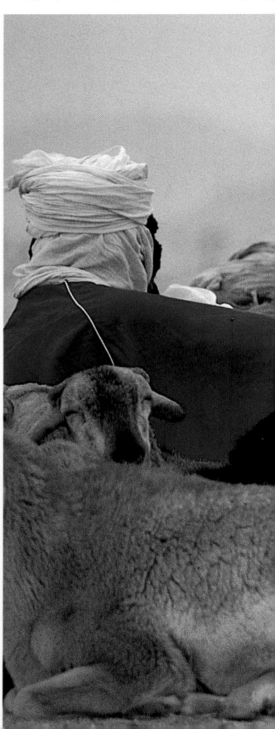

**54** Against the awe-inspiring backdrop of the Hoggar Mountains, Tuareg splash the neutral desert tones with specks of blue. Their nobility are descended from Berber stock and by marrying consistently within their own class, they have maintained their distinctive fair skin and fine features. Pride and prestige are paramount to the Tuareg. Out of respect, a stranger to an encampment wears his *tagilmust* so that his eyes peer from merest slits in the cloth. No man of any standing ever reveals his full face – even to friends – and in the past food and drink were taken beneath the veil.

They claim that only in the desert is a man truly free, and for many centuries they have been sole masters of this hostile territory. However, in the course of their wars and raids, they have won vassals and slaves of negroid stock and these people adopted Tamasheq – the language of the conquerors – and the desert as a home.

Essentially, the Tuareg are pastoralists. According to the territory they frequent, they keep camels and cattle, sheep and goats. Supremely sensitive to the needs of their herds and the scant resources of the Sahara, they move with confidence across its thirstland. Their diet is largely milk – soured, fresh, or dried and pounded with fruit into a crème. The desert's secret watering places are all known to them as are its fruits and grains. Many of their serfs and slaves remain at oases and cultivate dates and barley which the nobility, together with their entourages, collect as their due in the course of their long annual migrations.

But to the aristocracy, the most noble of the noble, such work is anathema and war is the only true vocation. Today these Tuareg find their activities curtailed by governments, their cattle raids outlawed, and the desert caravans taxed not by themselves but by customs officials. Their slaves have become educated and suddenly appear in the new bureaucracies as superiors to their erstwhile masters. These are strange and disquieting times for the Tuareg. Even the desert seems to have spurned them for the moment. Seven years of unremitting drought have driven the Tuareg, herdless, to the margins of the desert where they find themselves destitute and looked down upon.

But they know this drought will pass, and they look to the day when they will stride once more over the desert they love. Magnificent in his arrogance, the Tuareg spurns any world other than his own where he embodies man the opportunist. By exploiting every possible resource and linking his own lifestyle so intimately to his environment, his is, indeed, a rare freedom.

# West Africa

One of the most widely held misconceptions outside of Africa is that African societies were static. This is demonstrably untrue. West Africa in particular presents a long and exciting continuum of urban growth and cultural development going back to the first millennium and beyond.

Perhaps the greatest disadvantage in the study of Africa's past is the lack of written record, permitting distortion without the weight of documentary evidence to prove the contrary. The Nigerian scholar Dr Onwuka Dike aptly observes: 'The point is not that Africans have no history but that there is a profound ignorance concerning it, and an almost pathological unwillingness to believe the evidence when it is presented.'

However, even the earliest written records, those of Muslim travellers who crossed the Sahara and reached the great kingdoms of the Middle Niger, reflect these societies as dynamic and organised. The earlier history of this part of Africa is gradually being pieced together by archaeologists and their work, though incomplete, conclusively challenges any conception of a static civilization. Change indeed has been constant; continuous if often slow.

Between 6 000 and 4 000 years ago man in West Africa would have roamed over a far wider area than would be possible today. At that period in world climate the Sahara was not only relatively small but situated far north of its present position. Both the Sahelian zone, where semi-desert merges gradually into grassland proper, and the savannahs themselves, were probably far more extensive than is now the case.

We know that by at least some 4 000 years ago, man in this region of Africa had acquired cattle and, as the Sahara began to dry out and expand once more, he strode southwards driving his herds in search of pasture. In the course of his passage south, into what is now West Africa, he came up against an environmental barrier beyond which he could not go: the broad belt of tsetse fly infested country that cuts across West Africa from east to west. And just as those pastoralists of long ago were halted, so the movements southward of the Fulani today are inhibited.

This biting fly thrives in the hot, humid tropical zone and not only brings *nagana* to cattle but can infect man with sleeping sickness too. It presents an almost tangible barrier and even today in regions such as northern Nigeria the transition is abrupt: in one village

'Short of thermonuclear war itself, the problem of population growth is the gravest issue the world faces over the decades immediately ahead.'

Robert McNamara, President of the World Bank 1977

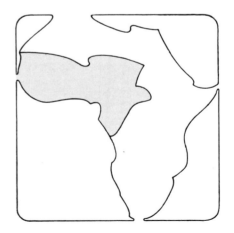

**55** Nets hang out to dry in this village in the lakes region of the Ivory Coast.

there will be the lowing of cattle, while in another, less than five kilometres away, there will be only the cackle of chickens and bleating of goats.

The Fulani are essentially cattle people and their great herds represent not only their main form of wealth, but indicate the status of the individual; if they are robust and healthy, he is seen as a responsible and hardworking man. Their success as pastoralists is largely due to their skilled management of their livestock which they lead along traditional routes from pasture to pasture according to the grasses and the seasons.

During the rains, the tsetse follow northwards the 1 000 millimetre isohyet which marks the rainfall limit of the fly. The Fulani therefore must move north too, to avoid the fly and at the same time take advantage of the fresh new growth of the season.

But when the dry season sets in, the tsetse retreat to wetter zones, allowing the Fulani to move back into land permanently occupied by cultivators. Once the harvest is in, the Fulani graze their herds on the stubble and the farmers in return get their fields manured. But the relationship goes beyond this: the Fulani trade meat, hides and dairy products with people such as the Hausa who live in the tsetse belt, and take grown foodstuffs in payment.

From the 13th century they began to convert to Islam, introduced to this part of Africa both by their Berber cousins and by Arabs involved in trans-Saharan trade: the new religion provided them with a new and dynamically unifying force. In the 19th century, under fanatical Muslim leaders, they set about conquering the infidel to their south. Fearless and inspired by their cause, these mounted fighting men overwhelmed their neighbours. Even now the Emirs of Timbuktu and Kano, Katsina and Sokoto are not Hausa, but Hausa-speaking Fulani. They asserted their dominance over both the rural peoples and those living in towns, but were entirely committed to their own culture. Those who remained to enjoy the spoils became a ruling élite, but the majority returned to the Sahelian zone to increase their cattle, their fortunes and their status. This, they say, is the life of a true Fulani.

In the past decade, especially in the years between 1972 and 1974, drought jeopardised their traditional way of life. They were cruelly squeezed between the implacable dryness of the advancing desert climate and their mortal enemy, the tsetse fly. The results have disrupted their nomadic existence and for many there is no going back. Some were able to compromise by acquiring land in the tsetse zone. Here they set up homesteads where their women till the fields to compensate with crops for the effects of the drought on their cattle. But these Fulani have not entirely lost their proud identity and the men still know the rigours of the herding life as they drive their much diminished cattle to scarce and distant pasture.

Not all have been so fortunate and been able to find land with which to make the transition to another lifestyle. In West Africa, the most heavily populated part of the continent, land – particularly fertile land – is at a premium. So many who had seen their drought-stricken herds reduced to piles of rotting carcasses have now come, destitute, to the towns where they struggle to adjust.

The Sahelian zone is the world of the pastoralist, but south of it the cultivator is supreme. When and whence cultivation reached this part of Africa is still uncertain. It is likely that the neolithic revolution travelled down the Nile Valley to beyond Khartoum, and there was adapted to millet and sorghum which are indigenous to Africa. The practice of cultivation, together with these crops, may well have then spread to West Africa by way of the Sahara's Sahelian fringe that straddles the continent from east to west.

Oral tradition in Benin lends authority to this suggestion, for J.V. Egharevba recorded: 'Many many years ago, the Binis came all the way from Egypt to found a more secure shelter in this part of the world after a short stay in the Sudan and at Ife-Ife, which the Benin people call Uhe. Before coming here, a band of hunters was sent to inspect this land and the report furnished was very favourable.'

Within the tropics the year is generally divided into the rainy seasons and the dry; of them, only the dry seasons can be counted on, as the rains are erratic and often late. Yet sorghum and millet are so well adapted to these conditions that they can survive an almost total wilt if the rains are late, and still recover to yield a reasonable harvest.

Whereas the indigenous African cereals flourished in fields cleared in the savannah, in the forests closer to the West African coast where rainfall increases markedly, the farmers learnt to clear

the trees and grow root crops such as cassava and yams. Recent studies of traditional methods in these productive areas reveal that the high yields are as much a result of careful and knowledgeable land use as of adequate rain and moderately good soils.

The origins of cultivation in West Africa are interesting from an academic point of view but the results are perhaps more relevant to the present situation.

The initial progression from a rural subsistence economy to one in which specialised crafts and surpluses are traded is not documented in West Africa. However, without doubt, this new way of life had a profound effect and set in motion the technological development that led to the urban cultures which so impressed foreigners who visited West Africa. The Moroccan traveller, Leo Africanus, reached Timbuktu in the 16th century and wrote: 'Here are many shops of artificers and merchants, and especially such as weave linen and cotton cloth. And hither do the Barbary merchants bring cloth to Europe . . . The inhabitants, and especially strangers there residing, are exceedingly rich . . . Here are great stores of doctors, judges, priests and other learned men, that are bountifully maintained at the king's costs and charges. And hither are brought divers manuscripts or written books out of Barbary which are sold for more money than other merchandise.'

Archaeologists have found evidence of iron-working in West Africa dating to about 2 500 years ago. This technology is believed to have originated in Assyria and been brought across the Mediterranean to the North African littoral where it may well have spread first westwards to what is now Morocco and then south to West Africa. It is also quite possible that the technology may have been brought directly from the north over the Sahara, for the paths and hidden watering places across its barren wastes have been known from earliest time.

Agriculture opened to man the humid tropical West African coast and the tsetse-infested savannah. Within the second half of the 1st millennium BC and the first centuries AD, the people of the brilliant civilizations of Nok and Ife in what is now central Nigeria were not only skilled cultivators but also leisured and sophisticated. While Europe lay shrouded in the Dark Ages, the artisans of Nok and Ife were creating magnificent naturalistic sculptures in bronze and terra cotta. And if we assume that the tastes and lifestyles of a people are reflected in the achievements of its art, then these sculptures must be the product of a highly developed African civilization.

Until the Portuguese outflanked the ancient trade routes over the desert and approached Africa from the sea in the early 1500s, the trans-Saharan connection dominated much of West Africa's early history. This part of the continent had always looked north beyond the desert for trade, and for the exchange of ideas and skills with the Berbers and the Arabs. Their inter-relationship can be traced back to the period when Egypt's rulers demanded new supplies of ivory and timber, slaves and gold. The Berbers and Arabs were the middlemen, trading with West African suppliers and then making the long and perilous journey across the Sahara to carry the goods to the constantly growing markets far away. The Romans imported African merchandise; they well appreciated leather made from the skins of goats from Katsina in what is now northern Nigeria, and brought to Morocco to be tanned and dyed – and from where they were exported as fine Moroccan leather.

In return for these items, West Africans obtained cloth and knives, horses and – above all – salt. With heavy rains continually leaching the West African soils, the entire ecosystem is deprived of sufficient salt: the plants, the animals and man himself. Animals go to salt licks to satisfy their wants; the West Africans traded gold and ivory for their supplies.

While the Berbers and the Arabs controlled the Mediterranean side of the trading relationship with Africa, kingdoms which also had as their economic base the trans-Saharan trade developed in the Middle Niger area.

The concept of trade on a local basis was already well-established over much of West Africa and had been closely linked to the developing urban centres, with markets as their focal points: and the inhabitants of scattered homesteads and villages must have realised the benefits of having recognised marketplaces to exchange goods.

Most people could produce enough to meet their immediate needs, but as tastes developed and there were the surpluses with which to trade, systems arose whereby different goods from many different regions could be exchanged: kola nuts and local cotton, gourds and pottery, knives and leatherware. There was also trade in foodstuffs.

The economic vitality of these urban centres in pre-colonial times seriously challenges those who perpetuate the myth of African 'backwardness'.

Today the marketplaces of countries such as Ghana, Nigeria, Senegal and the Gambia, Mali, Guinea and the Ivory Coast are dominated by women. In their spectacular and becoming cotton dresses – and with their babies on their backs – they conduct their daily business of buying and selling, bargaining and closing deals. The goods for sale indicate much of the changing tastes of West Africans and the ever-widening avenues of communication.

The Hausa, five and a half million today, reveal the influences and effects of a long history of commerce, technological development and urban growth – they also reflect the powerful force of Islam in this part of Africa.

The new religion reached West Africa through the Berbers and the Arabs with whom the local Africans had well-established trading relationships. Indeed the introduction of Islam to West Africa had as much to do with the needs of commerce as with religion. The historian A.G. Hopkins points out that 'three chief requirements of long distance trade were capital, credit and security'. It had become vital that there should be some mutually recognised code of honour between businessmen, and Islam provided it.

By the 13th century its impact had spread westwards through North Africa, along the bulge and from there reached the commercial centres of the Middle Niger. Its spiritual attractions to the people of West Africa have been much debated but doubtless it offered pragmatic advantages as well, not the least of which was the Arab and Berber preference for dealings based on mutually recognised guarantees with fellow Muslims who shared the common allegiance to Allah.

Islamic schools set up in the larger centres offered the sons of local Africans the opportunity to join a broader religious community and an entrée to a ruling class: and it is scarcely surprising that Islam was widely adopted by – and in some degree adapted to – the traditional cultures of people such as the Hausa who were already involved with trade. Even today it is a powerful force binding many West Africans, both French and English speaking.

The Muslim Hausa also well-illustrate that there was a marked degree of urbanisation in pre-industrial Africa, with highly organised infra-structures of centralised government and urban amenities. Kano was by no means the only metropolis: other centres such as Gao, Djenne and Timbuktu in the 15th and 16th centuries had populations of between 15 000 and 80 000. Indeed, almost half the population of Hausaland was urban. In the 19th century, further south in the forested areas there were also towns of considerable size in Yorubaland which boasted at least 10 with populations of more than 20 000. At Abidjan, within walls 39 kilometres in length, some 70 000 citizens were engaged in an orderly and prosperous way of life.

At an early stage of growth the buildings clustered round the marketplace would have been mud-walled and thatch-roofed. In time, however, when the increase of population demanded amenities such as water and properly constructed drainage and waste disposal systems, the authorities had to impose building regulations, for in densely packed urban areas thatch becomes a fire hazard and waste disposal has to be controlled.

Within the towns there were specialists of every kind – metal workers and butchers, weavers and saddlers, barber-surgeons and herbalists, traders and agents – at every level there was a high degree of technological self-sufficiency. But most important of all was food. Most townsmen were farmers as well who devoted some of their energies – and their women's hard work – to the production of at least enough food to provide for the basic daily needs of the family; surpluses were traded for luxuries and for foodstuffs they did not produce themselves.

West Africa is not particularly fertile and there are large areas of poor soils. Furthermore, as one moves north from the sub-equatorial and tropical zones bordering on the Gulf of Guinea and the Atlantic, there is a gradual decrease in rain until, in what are now the giant territories of Mauritania, Mali, Niger and Chad, it ceases altogether and the desert tightens its grip. West Africa's vegetation as well as its climate reflects this remarkable zonal arrangement and nowhere in Africa is the sequence of latitude more apparent.

The tropical and sub-equatorial regions which run close to and parallel with the coast are the most productive areas, but they are also plagued by such tropical scourges as malaria, bilharzia and river blindness; debilitating, if not fatal, diseases that seriously affect the productivity of the people. River blindness, carried by the black fly *Simulium damnosum,* afflicts at least a million in the Volta River basin alone.

A pamphlet entitled 'Stemming the River of Darkness' well illustrates the terrible effects of this disease: 'The human tragedy is coupled with an economic one. If you fly over the worst onchocerciasis (river blindness) regions, you see green, well-watered land that looks ideal for agriculture and animal raising. But you see little sign of man. When you do, it will be a deserted village, grass-roofing collapsed and mud walls crumbling. Along the White Volta alone, some 50 villages are abandoned.

'Having been forced to surrender their fertile land to the black fly, people crowd on to the plateau, where uncertain rains and thin soils produce violent fluctuations in crop yields. Much of the plateau land should not be farmed at all, but retained as forest reserve. Soil exhaustion and erosion, then follow' where farming is practised. In some of these areas blindness is so universal that the people cannot believe that this is not the way of the world at large.

In terms of mortality, disease is often the mechanism which brings death rather than its direct cause. This is particularly apparent today when the effects and stresses of high density living – such as malnutrition, poor hygiene and inadequate resources – leave the population vulnerable to illnesses.

The Portuguese were the first Europeans to arrive on the West African coast. In their tiny ships they battled the unknown seas, rounding the bulge in their bid for the Indies. However they were well aware that West Africa was rich in gold, for amazing tales had reached them of how the ruler of the kingdom of Mali, Mansa Musa, had lavished gold on the populace of Cairo and elsewhere as he passed through on his way to Mecca. On their way to the East the Portuguese hoped to secure some of this wealth – or at least initiate relationships that would lead to this.

They found the coastline dangerously inhospit-

able; for as the Sahara guarded the northern entry to West Africa, so the sea buttressed the south. Indeed, it had only two natural harbours at what are now Dakar and Freetown. For the remainder, the shore is flat and straight with sandbanks enclosing lagoons behind which the rivers such as the mighty Niger and Senegal reach the sea. But contact was made, and the effects were to grow and multiply as the centuries passed.

Essentially the early relationship was based on mutual reward. The Portuguese primarily sought gold and slaves; the African people at the coast wanted salt and horses, weapons and cloth. And as the potential for economic gain became more apparent to the African traders at the coast, so they began to wrest control of merchandise from the older, better-established kingdoms to their north which in turn began to experience a decline in revenue – and in power.

The gold trade now passed through the hands of a new generation of men, and slaves were becoming an even more valuable commodity. Europe was just beginning to open up the New World and she needed men to work the sugarfields and plantations of the Americas.

Strengthened by the arms they were receiving in return for gold, ivory and slaves, highly organised groups such as the Manding and Malinke became dominant. Their raids against others gained a fresh impetus and earlier territorial imperatives were now overtaken by the profit motive.

Between 1700 and 1810 over three million of the strongest men and women were transplanted as slaves under inhuman conditions, mainly to the New World. By this time Britain, France and Holland had entirely eclipsed the earlier Portuguese traders along what has become notorious as the 'Slave Coast', from where researchers estimate that in all as many as 10 million slaves were taken.

Prior to this appalling period in West African history, population growth, in spite of the effects of endemic disease on the death rate, particularly that of infants, had risen slowly but steadily. The plentiful food supply had further helped increase the longevity of the population as a whole. And in terms of the agricultural technology available and the requirements of what was essentially shifting cultivation, the limits on available land must have been becoming uncomfortably apparent. In the internal conflicts that preceded the arrival of the

European, land may well have been a central issue.

Contact with the outside world, particularly with regions of similar climate in South America, introduced several new food crops to West Africa – maize and tobacco, tomatoes and pineapples, and a host of other useful and productive plants. These were readily adopted by West African farmers and spread inland where they provided the variety which prevents total famine if conditions do not favour the one or two crops previously cultivated. To some extent the improved nutrition may have increased the ability of the population to withstand disease, thus compensating its depletion through slavery. On the other hand, the prime targets of the slavers were men in their prime and healthy women of childbearing age whose loss would both adversely affect the number of children born and also manpower to work the village fields.

These were dark and frightening years during which the powerful few grew rich and the majority lived in fear and uncertainty. In the 1700s, one group began to gain ascendancy over the rest in terms of trade: the Ashanti. They were basically composed from several weak and distantly related groups in what is now Ghana. In self-defence against the depredations of more powerful neighbours, they joined together and, under several astute leaders, gradually won almost total control of the gold and slave trade in West Africa.

Their kings, the *Asantehene*, took as symbol of power the Golden Stool. Stools of various materials, but mainly wood, were owned by chiefs and village heads and were symbols of authority. However, the significance of the stool was for long entirely misunderstood by Europeans who came into contact with the Ashanti. They realised that it was a symbol of the supreme power of the *Asantehene* but they sought a parallel in their own cultures. In 1900 when Britain tired of dealing through the Ashanti, she determined to bring them under the yoke of the Empire, and sent out Sir Frederick Hodgson to enlighten them as to her might. In his ignorance he demonstrated in what he believed to be the most telling way, the supremacy of the British monarch; he sat on the Golden Stool. He had not understood that no-one, not even the *Asantehene,* ever sat on the stool for it was believed to embody the very spirit of the Ashanti people.

This shocked them into action. Their national pride demanded redress and they embarked upon a year of bloody conflict with the British. More and more reinforcements were sent out from England, and eventually the superior fire-power prevailed, but at great cost in human lives on both sides. The Ashanti not only lost the war, but subsequently found that their traditional sources of gold had finally run out and that other people were now dealing directly with the Europeans.

Trade and commercial dealings along the coast had already assumed a new and different tenor as a direct result of events in Europe. The industrial revolution of the 19th century had thrust countries such as France, Britain and Germany into a new era with new economic realities. Keystones to this development had been a spate of inventions and discoveries that transformed their former agrarian economies into industrial ones.

The industrial revolution completely restructured European society; urbanisation and industrialisation became the new watchwords. Inherent in these developments was also a commitment to growth with which to sustain industry – and also to its concomitant, exploitation. Of course they were not seen that way in Europe at the time.

Britain recognised that she would have to look beyond her shores for the raw materials to keep her factories going, and West Africa, so conveniently close, was an obvious source. Later still, her peoples came to represent to Britain – and the rest of the industrial world – a potential market for cloth and steel and a plethora of manufactured goods from hatchets to rifles and dress lengths.

The technology that provided Europe with the advantages of industrialization went to her head: during this time there was a growing belief among Europeans that their industrial revolution had not only won them economic power but had simultaneously imbued them with a moral superiority. With this two-headed weapon, colonialism was inflicted upon Africa.

In their earlier relationship with West Africans, Europeans had recognised the authority of local rulers and their sovereignty. This now took on a new dimension, for the industrialists saw that the most advantageous way in which to gain access to resources was to take possession of them. Furthermore, in the spirit of competition between European countries all rushing pell-mell along the road

to greater industrial development and growth, it became economically sensible to stake your claims on Africa's soil – and then defend them with the gun.

From the start the emphasis was on the provision of raw material for the industrialised world. African farmers were encouraged to grow groundnuts and rubber, cocoa and coffee; food production for local markets took second place to the far more profitable cash crops. Timber, cotton, palm oil were shipped out of West Africa. In the 20th century when her mineral wealth – such as diamonds, iron ore and bauxite – began to be exploited, they too were sent to Europe.

But there were benefits other than cash profits for West Africans. Western technology initially improved their lives; most of all medicine, which for the first time offered cures and control of the ancient tropical diseases. Literacy, previously introduced with Islam, now reached a greater number, giving skills and the key to improved technology.

But there were also the seeds of future problems, dimly perceived but taking root. And when, in the 1950s and 1960s independence came to the West African world, the bitter fruits began to appear.

Since independence, West African countries have tended to ship raw materials overseas in the same way that they did as the colonies of foreign powers. The political independence has not been paralleled by economic independence and industrial development has been slow. The sort of diversified industries producing goods suited specially to the needs and tastes of local markets have been slow in coming. Indeed, much of the technology imported to this part of the world is still aimed at using cheap labour to produce goods for foreign markets.

Urban migration also took on a new – and increasing – tempo. West Africa accounts for approximately a fifth of Africa's land surface and yet she contains more than 100 million people – over a third of the continent's population. In Lagos alone there are more than a million and the influx continues daily. Abidjan doubled its population between 1961 and 1968 to half a million. More than 10 per cent of Senegal's peoples live in Dakar.

Traditionally West Africans were agriculturalists and the principle of self-sufficiency always applied. A man planted first of all to feed his family; beyond that he planted for profit. The development of cash crop farming with an eye to overseas markets is a legacy of the colonial period and one which many West African farmers have not yet managed to discard. When world prices are high, they stand to do extremely well – in fact far better than they would do selling chillis and millet at the local market. However, when world prices for commodities such as cocoa or groundnuts or palm oil drop, then the African farmer finds himself at the mercy of markets over which he has little or no control.

In West Africa today greater emphasis is being placed on providing crops for local markets and, where possible, local industries to offset the effects of these unaccountable and uncontrollable changes in world prices.

Some have done well out of the land but this is the exception rather than the rule. Families have grown, the availability of land has decreased, and productivity has declined under the pressure. Even the much-vaunted 'Green Revolution' imported from the West, failed to stem the tide, for although the new hybrids are high-yielding, they are vulnerable to drought and pests, and require inputs of fertilizer, pesticides and technology far beyond the reach of the small farmer. The alternative for many is to seek better fortunes in the towns.

How will the West African urban dweller make a living? Where can he best employ his energies? It is difficult to find answers to these questions, for the cities and towns can neither sustain him nor offer him employment. In the vast slums and squatter camps that surround most of the urban areas, there is an abysmal lack of basic facilities such as water, sanitation, medical care, education and proper housing. Most of all, there is a lack of any opportunity to earn a decent living.

Close behind the problem of urban migration is another interrelated one: the spectre of a soaring population growth rate. It is still common for a woman to produce a child every four years in the rural areas, and in the towns where the traditional family structure and attitudes to the spacing of children are seriously eroded, she may bring a new mouth into the world every two years.

It is not simply enough for the principles of birth control to be entrenched either voluntarily or by law. There must be a multi-faceted approach aimed at educating as many people as possible with new skills aimed primarily at producing food and goods for the home market.

And in our finite world, it is clearly apparent that resources such as the copper, iron, oil, bauxite and diamonds with which West Africa is amply blessed, will also be depleted one day. The foreign earnings, from these exports are largely sustaining the current standard of living: But what of tomorrow? Where are Nigeria's future petrochemical industries to purchase oil if she exhausts her present supplies? We can no longer plan just for today and assume that we can deal with tomorrow's problems when we get there.

The politicians and the rulers will need strong nerves – and all their gifts of persuasion – to win for their people a better future, for often the long-term solutions are extremely unattractive, particularly with the western industrialised countries offering such tantalising examples of living standards to which West Africans, too, would like to aspire. The sad reality is that for the majority, these dreams – or even a far more modest way of life – are an impossibility.

**56** Lithe and easy and undisturbed by her suckling infant, a Fulani girl carries calabashes to market.

**57, 58** Occupying a broad belt of land across national boundaries from Senegal in the west over the continent to the Sudan in the east, are the Fulani – six million people bound together by a common tongue, Fulfulde, and by values that set them apart from the other peoples of West Africa. They are further distinguished by their Caucaso-negroid appearance which they enhance with cosmetics and ornaments. These women have worked coins and tokens into their hair, while others lengthen it with twine before wrapping it in brass wire and decking it with jewellery.

**59** Splendid gold earrings, typical of the Fulani, weigh down the lobes. This woman wears a sling across the top of her head to help support earrings which will become larger as her husband's wealth increases and more of the precious metal is beaten into them. Her bold amber beads are also highly valued and popular.

57
58  60
59

**60** The Fulani say 'see the nose, know the man', for they maintain that one whose nose is short and straight and whose lips are finely drawn will automatically embody those virtues which they hold most high. Such a person, they say, is truly Fulani. Through consistent interbreeding, the aristocracy has retained these elegant features.

Resplendent at a feast, this Fulani youth includes poetry and dancing among his accomplishments.

**61, 62** Pastoralism in West Africa is synonymous with the Fulani. They lead their herds of zebu cattle from pasture to pasture between the emptiness of the Sahara to the north and the tsetse-infested lands of the West African savannah.

**63** On a visit to Gao, a Fulani herdsman wears traditional headgear and optical hardware.

In the late 18th and early 19th centuries, outstanding Fulani leaders conquered the entire Middle Niger area, urging their men in the name of Mohammed to vanquish the morally lax and the infidel. With victory, most Fulani returned by choice to pastoralism, leaving an élite to exercise power in the towns and cities such as Gao, Kano, Sokoto and Katsina.

*Following page* (64): Djenne mosque, serene and powerful above the market's bustle, is perhaps the most outstanding example of its kind in West Africa, combining as it does the spiritual impact of Islam with African symbolism and architectural traditions. The studded effect comes from numerous split timbers necessary to support such lofty mud walls and the spiral staircases inside the minarets. The jutting spires which are part of the façade echo the phallic symbol on the building visible in the left foreground.

76

61
62 63

**68, 69, 70** In painted masks, brightly coloured straw skirts and breastplates of cowrie shells, the Dogon Society of the Mask gathers for a funeral.

*Following page* (71): Tall granaries tucked precariously against the cliff faces incorporate in their architectural features the Dogon conception of the cosmos. Griaule explained: 'the four uprights ending in the corners of the square roof were the arms and legs.' On another plane, he said, the granary could be seen as 'a woman lying on her back (representing the sun) with her arms and legs raised supporting the roof (representing the sky). The two legs were on the north side, and the door at the sixth step marked the sexual parts.'

68   69                                                          70

83

**72** Spear and clothing balanced on his head, a man paddles on a log float along the southern shore of Lake Chad. Rarely more than two metres deep, this great expanse of tepid water shrinks and grows with the seasons, doubling in size to 25 000 square kilometres after the rains. But viewed over a two-million-year time span, the lake is a mere fraction of its former self – and still dwindling. Today, the seasonal *Harmattan* winds drive desert sands into the water, threatening finally to smother this ancient lake which some 10 000 years ago extended far into what is now the Sahara.

**73** These sun-dried fish are destined for distant West African markets.

**74** Dug-out canoes splayed along Lake Chad's shore are baled out in preparation for the day's fishing.

*Following page* (75): At the height of the dry season, fire and sun scorched this gaunt landscape in the Mandara Mountains of Cameroon. Three weeks later the first rains fell, transforming the land with a delicate flush of green.

72 73
74

**76** Fecundity, diligence, modesty – and a strong pair of arms – are the attributes of a good wife over much of Africa. Women are a vital element in the traditional workforce. Despite their talent for making light of hard work, they toil long hours in the fields and are expected to care for hearth and home. But they are not slaves and their rights are protected by the traditions of their society.

Polygamy – having more than one wife – was never as widespread in Africa as popularly believed in the West, for only relatively few men were well-off enough to be able to afford the bridewealth for more than one wife – or for her upkeep.

These wives of a Sirigu tribesman spend their leisure in the immaculate courtyard of their home, making sturdy baskets for sale. The income will belong to them to spend as they wish.

**77** Interlocking forms and contrasting textures of a Sirigu homestead.

**78** A century ago the decorations on this cap were money, for the cowrie shell was standard currency throughout much of West Africa.

The cowrie shell – like the $10 bill – has little intrinsic value, but the fact that it is easy to handle and count, is durable and almost impossible to counterfeit, probably explains its widespread acceptance as currency, not only in this part of Africa, but in many other parts of the world as well.

Originally cowries came to West Africa from the Indian Ocean islands via North Africa and the Middle East and were the 'small change' in the system where gold represented the 'big bills'.

Later, European traders to Africa brought huge quantities of cowries for their business dealings with the natives, but the black middlemen soon realised that the cowrie no longer filled its former functions: both sides did not value it equally and gradually it was relegated to the decorative.

*Following page* (79): At the signal, hundreds of men plunge into the river at Argungu for the annual fishing competition. Calabash floats are part of their equipment.

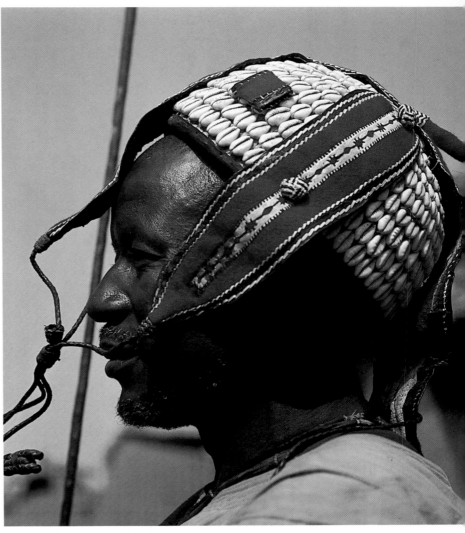

94

81  82

*Previous page* (80): Suffused with evening light, washing draped over bushes dries on the outskirts of Kano, one of the most important of the original seven Hausa city states.

When the traveller Heinrich Barth reached Kano in 1851 he found it to be a city enclosed in mud walls 20 kilometres long, 13 metres thick and with 15 heavily guarded entrances.

**81** Splendidly attired and mounted, a drummer in the Emir of Katsina's procession marks the end of the Islamic month of fasting, Ramadan.

**82** Preceded by magnificent entourages, dignitaries on their way to Kano's *Durbar* festival for Muslim horsemen, parade on mounts caparisoned in gold through streets thronging with Hausa citizens. Once the procession passed, people returned to their normal activities as merchants, traders and specialist craftsmen.

Kano's commercial vitality is not a new phenomenon. Long before the first European had ventured into this part of Africa, the city was a highly organised – and highly successful – trading centre. But the Hausa were not simply middlemen. On the basis of their efficient use of the land they had been able to produce food surpluses and no doubt this in itself attracted people from other areas to do business. By 999 AD when Kano's recorded history begins, the Hausa were clearly also taking advantage of their position at one of the most important crossroads for trans-Saharan trade.

The Hausa, however, had even more to offer. In the urban centres developing around markets they began to apply the ideas and technology brought by traders from North Africa. Most successful of all was their textile industry based on local cotton dyed the famous indigo blue. When Heinrich Barth reached this metropolis in 1851 he estimated the export trade in cloth alone was worth about three hundred million cowries – roughly the equivalent of $100 000 today.

**83** Patiently waiting for customers, a calabash vendor bedecked in solid gold, sits in the hot sun at a market in the Middle Niger region.

**84** Against the babble of the market-place, women drive hard bargains.

The West African market system has been built up over many centuries and is at once specialised and cosmopolitan. This section of Zinder market sells pots and gourds but elsewhere customers can buy anything from English-manufactured cloth and torchlight batteries to locally grown chillis and Moroccan leather, at prices which are set each day. Children transmit the going rates all over town, learning early the cut and thrust of commerce and trade.

While some of his produce may well find its way into the family cooking pots, wherever possible, the West African farmer grows crops that will yield the best financial return. With his eye on the market-place, he caters to demand and uses the profits to buy items he either cannot produce himself or which are more economical for him to buy from others.

*Previous page* (85): Good husbandry and prosperity create a mosaic of well-tilled fields and neatly thatched homesteads in this Nigerian rural landscape. Not all of West Africa is particularly fertile but ingenuity and skill have made it agriculturally productive, for the tsetse fly renders much of this region unsuited to cattle herding.

Whereas the savannahs of East and southern Africa lend themselves to pastoralism, West Africa's relatively fertile soils and good rainfall suit the cultivator. These farmers know their land and use it admirably, manuring the fields, rotating crops and leaving areas fallow. And while their methods do not produce the staggering yields of the Saskatchewan wheat farmer, their system requires little in the way of tools, machines, chemical fertilizers and pesticides – yet is both profitable and self-sustaining.

**86** Surrounded by some of the symbols of his former power, a deposed Bamileke chief poses stiffly with his old and trusted servant (seated right) and his only remaining counsellor.

**87** Twelve women share this large kitchen in a north Cameroon homestead. The equipment includes a sturdy crushing table, cupboard, special storage areas under the thatch roof, and a fireplace.

88

89

**88** This replica of a Benin ivory mask in the British Museum became the symbol of Festac, the spectacular arts festival held in Lagos in 1977.

**89** New freedoms and contacts with the outside world are reflected in this expressive modern sculpture at Oshogo.

**90** In the past, African sculptural forms were essentially conservative, having changed little over the centuries. This carved figure in traditional style underlines the African ideal of fertility and the fathering of many children.

**91** A Senegalese woman, educated, sophisticated and a member of Africa's urban élite.

**92** Lagos's distant skyscrapers reflect the tremendous wealth generated by oil-rich Nigeria – in sharp contrast to the poverty of the many who have come, hopeful, to the city to share in the national bonanza.

Urban migration presents modern Africa with some of

her thorniest problems. The migrants are motivated primarily by the belief that the towns and cities offer them greater opportunities and rewards than does a rural existence. For the young people – particularly those with some education – the towns promise excitement, new freedoms and, most important of all, more money. The reality is far from this. Unemployed and disaffected, they find themselves in the shanty towns which have become such a common feature of African urban life.

This situation has arisen in part from economic patterns established during colonial times when the industrialised nations of the world began to extract Africa's raw materials, exploiting her labour. And, in the wake of independence, few countries have been able to break these patterns successfully. They have remained dependent on the export of one or two primary products, unable to diversify the economy and generate employment opportunities by which the natural wealth could reach the majority of the people.

But while governments are being urged to search for solutions that are both equitable and effective, the migrants still stream to the towns, creating potentially explosive social and political situations.

**93** Waste gas flares from one of Nigeria's oil wells.

*Previous page* (94): To the steady beat of a drum, rowers plunge their oars into the water at a regatta held during Festac in Lagos, 1977.

**95** Calabashes are the favourite 'shopping bags' of West African women who carry them nonchalantly on their heads over long distances. Since food spoils rapidly in the heat and humidity, they come daily to the markets. Here they also buy new calabashes as basins and bowls, and have their old ones fixed by the calabash menders who sew up the cracks with plant fibre.

**96** For the traditional naming ceremony of her niece, this young woman has had her hair specially styled. It is a time-consuming process and women take hours dressing one another's hair. First the existing style is teased out with a long-toothed comb and the hair is finely parted. The short curly strands are lengthened with cotton or string, oiled and then plaited into new styles, artistic and becoming.

**97** Toting their ever-present babies, Ghanaian women buy tomatoes at a crowded market.

The tomato, like the pineapple and pawpaw, is not an African fruit but a highly successful transplant brought by Portuguese voyagers from similar environments in Central and South America. Whereas Africans took quickly to the exotic tomato, Europeans treated it with the utmost suspicion. They considered it poisonous and ignored it for almost 200 years until the publication in 1822 of a paper extolling its virtues.

In Africa, however, maize and manioc were far more significant introductions from tropical America than the tomato. Both were nutritious alternatives to the indigenous millet and yam and broadened the spectrum of staples, in turn providing better insurance against famine.

While diet and population growth are closely linked, the fact that a third of Africa's people live in West Africa cannot be entirely credited to better eating. The reasons for the present numbers are often difficult to trace and explain for they are invariably the result of a subtle interplay of factors such as environment, history, politics and the survival strategies adopted by different peoples.

However, comparatively speaking, cultivation supports a far greater population than, say, pastoralism or a hunter-gatherer existence and this must account to some extent for the concentration of peoples historically associated with this part of Africa.

110

95

96

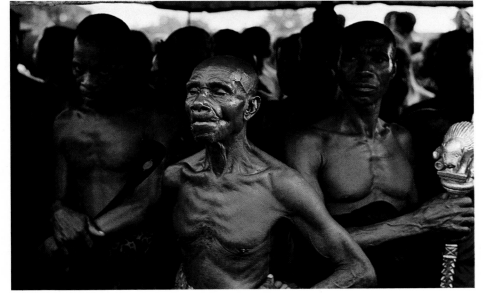

*Previous page* (100): Keening and wailing in their brilliant mourning dress, Ashanti women lament the death of their King in 1970.

**101** The drums that 'speak' to the people are part of an elaborate and ritualised set of beliefs developed by the Ashanti leaders to bind their people together.

**102** Smoking cigarettes while they play a traditional game, Ashanti nobles relax.

**103** To the cries of *ti ye* ('listen') the traditional council of the Ashanti meets to discuss matters affecting its people. The new *Asantehene* or King, the 19th in a dynasty that goes back to the beginning of the 17th century, presides under the great umbrella that signifies his supreme rank. His is the final word in any matter.

**104** An elderly chieftain attends the funeral ceremonies of the old *Asantehene.* He cannot remember 1900 when the terrible year-long war between Britain and his people brought to an end 200 years of Ashanti rule.

The Ashanti arose from oppression to become oppressors in their turn. They were originally groups of weak related peoples who joined together to defend themselves against strong neighbours. Under able and ambitious leaders they were forged into a strong military nation, well-placed as entrepreneurs trading the gold of the hinterland with the Europeans at the coast.

From the outset gold and the Ashanti were closely associated. Slaves were used to pan the alluvial gold from rivers and dig the precious nuggets from the earth. And when it became apparent that there was further wealth to be made in selling slaves to European buyers at the coast, they entered this trade as well.

By the mid-18th century, virtually the entire West African slave and gold trade was in Ashanti hands. But the rival imperialisms of the Ashanti and the British were destined to conflict and at the beginning of the 20th century the Ashanti, after much bloodshed, were subjugated and added to the British Empire. Today the Ashanti farm cocoa and their kingdom is part of West Africa's dynamic past.

**101  102**

**103**

**104**

**105**

**105** The catch is in, gutted and drying. All along West Africa's coast dried fish are marketed on the beach.

**106** At St Louis on the estuary of the Senegal River, the beach is a favourite meeting-place of the men who exchange news and make business deals there.

West Africans are not great seafarers, but they know their treacherous coast with its sandbars, dangerous currents and lack of harbours. These must have been frustrating for the Europeans probing the West African coast for safe harbour and foothold on the continent. It is unlikely, however, that they were real deterrents. Had the mariners of the 16th and 17th centuries required Africa's resources – or even perceived the full potential of the interior of the 'dark continent' – not even malaria and local hostility would have kept them out.

As it was they were satisfied to deal in gold, slaves and ivory with the people along the coast, bringing trade

goods such as horses, foodstuffs and beads in return.

But during the 19th century this relationship between equals began to change. The Industrial Revolution had transformed Britain's rural economy and she was caught up in the complexities of urbanisation and industrialisation. And with the economic realities of this new system came new pressures which impelled Europeans on a search for raw materials and new markets. The ships that set out heavily laden with iron pots from Birmingham and dress lengths from Manchester returned equally heavily laden with raw materials to stoke the industrial furnace.

It was but a short step from haggling with the black middlemen who supplied these raw materials to claiming them for yourself. With competition rife between the industrial powers of Europe, staking out a share of Africa and defending it seemed sound economic sense. Colonialism in Africa had begun.

**107** Cloaked in lush green and interlaced with waterways, this tropical African landscape appears superlatively fertile and productive.

Agriculturalists had been convinced that such luxuriant growth must spring from rich soils. But when they cleared the forest and planted crops, they were surprised to find that the soils of tropical Africa are extremely poor. It only then became apparent that whatever nutrients the soil contained had been fully taken up by the existing trees and undergrowth: little had been left unused in the soil. With every massive tree that had been felled and shipped overseas, had gone most of the vital nutrients of the forest.

Armed with this knowledge, developers have a choice: they can either exploit Africa's tropical forest wisely so that its productivity is sustained – or ignore the warnings and destroy it forever.

**108** In Central Africa's tropical forest, a Pygmy mother and her infant wear coloured pigments on their faces to ward off danger. Like his parents, this baby is unlikely to grow more than 1,5 metres tall.

How the Pygmies came to make their home in the forest is not known.

**109** Attracted by a movement in the foliage, this Pygmy lad prepares to shoot.

**110** The Pygmies say that a hungry Pygmy is a lazy Pygmy, for the forest provides them freely with everything they really need. These men have killed an elephant which had wandered into their territory.

**111** In Africa only the Pygmy feels secure and unoppressed in such a setting. Other peoples who have been forced to make clearings to grow crops along the edges of the forest consider it grudging, even malevolent.

The relationship between these two groups of people is an expression of their diametrically opposed attitudes to this environment; yet the symbiosis between them was long misunderstood. In the presence of the taller black cultivators, the Pygmy seems menial and subservient, giving forest produce and labour for apparently little return. Recent studies have shown, however, that the Pygmy is a willing participant in the relationship, and has chosen to provide outsiders with the produce of the forest, thereby deterring them from entering his domain.

110

111

*Previous page* (112): The flesh of two wild pigs killed by Pygmy hunters is wrapped in large leaves and carried in special slings to the nearby encampment. Not only does the forest provide meat, but with little effort the women find in it a wealth of mushrooms, fruit, nuts and roots to enrich the diet.

**113** Broad river highway to the interior, the Zaire River penetrates some 4 700 kilometres into Central Africa. The lower stretches of the river and their lazy-flowing tributaries are navigable but cataracts and rapids make the higher reaches useless for rivercraft.

**114** Despite their immense size – a large male can weigh a thousand kilograms – gorillas climb trees to feed, relax and build the nests in which they sleep at night. But the huge mineral potential of the Zaire Basin has drawn people into the gorilla's home ranges; in the face of these intrusions this shy creature has retreated and is now an endangered species.

113   114

127

# East Africa

Photographs of the earth taken by orbiting satellite reveal the Great Rift Valley as an unhealed slash-wound down the face of Africa. From the Red Sea in the north the Rift runs parallel to the East African coast for more than 9 500 kilometres to Lake Malawi, and its influence reaches beyond as far as Botswana's Mgadigadi salt pans.

Africa is being torn apart by the same primal forces that split the ancient southern landmass of Gondwanaland, leaving Africa as the stable core and setting free, in a slow slide east, south and west, immense fragments which eventually settled to become the other southern continents – Antarctica, South America and Australia.

The Great Rift Valley is not the result of a single cataclysmic occurrence but rather the result of gradual build-ups and releases of pressures along a set of parallel fractures in the earth's crust. In the course of many millions of years the land between these fractures slipped down, leaving the distinctive Rift Valley features of today.

Over the past 11 million years since the main faulting took place there has been continuous geological movement – as recently as a million years ago the shoulders of the valley were further uplifted in places and new faulting occurred on its floor. Even now there are 30 active volcanoes along the Rift and the ancient cones and lava flows of many more have left their mark both in physical relics and in the chemical components of East Africa's soils. From the Danakil Depression in the north come reports of violent earthquakes, and far to the south, deep beneath Botswana's Okavango swamps, the earth shudders in response to subterranean forces still at work.

This immense gash, of impressive magnitude even when seen from outer space, has had a proportionately great influence on the ground, and in East Africa along its length it determines the lives of men.

To traverse the Great Rift Valley is still to experience something of primordial Africa, an Africa little touched by the outside world. In its far north man's presence is hardly evident, for this region is so hostile that few choose to venture there. The Danakil Desert is a blasted hellhole where the land dips to 150 metres below sea level and the heat is unremitting. Harsh salt flats are interspersed with strange volcanic outcrops and only at its southern end is there water where the Awash River flows down from the Ethiopian highlands to wallow finally to its death in the desert.

Here live the Afar, some 200 000 in all and as fierce as their surroundings. The Awash is the key to their survival and they stay close

*'Man has come from bewilderment through knowledge to truculence and the brink of self-destruction. To survive, he must add understanding of himself to knowledge of his environment.'*

*G.C. Last* Man and Africa *1965*

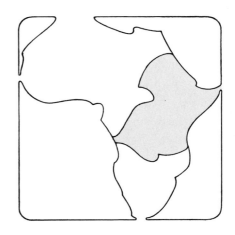

**115** Pounding hooves raise the dust as zebra gallop over the savannah.

to its banks, each group jealously guarding its rights to water. Most of them are herdsmen, and eke a living from the meagre pastures, while some mine the salt of the desert.

The Danakil salt is evidence of its past when it was part of the Red Sea. As recently as 10 000 years ago fish were swimming here; and then the earth buckled, throwing up a ridge of hills in the north where the Danakil meets the sea. Behind this barrier, intense sunlight evaporated the water, leaving the crust of salt that the Afar hack into blocks and take to the markets of the more hospitable regions of Ethiopia.

Rain in the Danakil is rare, but the western and southern parts of Ethiopia's highlands are pounded by summer rains which not only leach much of the mineral nutrients from the earth but also erode the topsoil and carry it away in a rich red torrent to the Nile in the west, to the Awash, and to the river systems of her East African neighbours to the south. In the sheer force of their fall, the rainstorms of tropical Africa have always ripped away the earth unless their impact is broken by a layer of trees, shrubs and grasses. In Ethiopia this protective covering of plant life is being removed at a dangerous rate. The pressures of too many people on the land are readily apparent in the erosion which has left once productive regions barren. These effects are particularly severe in Ethiopia, which is essentially mountainous with a tormented relief to encourage rapid run-off. Without the benefit of the roots and stems of plants to hold the rainfall long enough to let it percolate downwards, gravity washes the water swiftly down into the valleys and away. At the end of the seven dry months between November and May the Ethiopians await the rains that will bring life and nurture the newly-planted crops and replenish the pastures. Today, their arrival does as much harm as good in the regions where man's demands have been greatest.

But while Ethiopia constitutes a dramatic example of the destructive power of water, it is not unique on the African continent: from the Sudan to Kenya and southwards to the eastern parts of South Africa, the earth bears the sterile scars that result from a process too often begun by man. The basic elements in the scenario are a rapidly increasing human population and land whose limits are invariably over-strained.

With the increase in the number of mouths to feed, people look to the land to find more of the essentials for survival: food, water and firewood. Almost 90 per cent of Ethiopians are still on the land; they practise an ancient tradition of agriculture in which crops are rotated and fields left fallow to regain their strength, and the steep slopes are carefully terraced to prevent erosion. Herds of cattle are pastured on the highlands and the ubiquitous goat flourishes on the poorer land.

The Ethiopians developed these methods slowly, learning by trial and error which gave the best return for their efforts. And for many centuries their choices stood them in good stead.

The Ethiopians are not homogenous although most speak Amharic. Over half belong to the Galla, Somali and Afar groups which are in themselves a mixture. Almost certainly they reflect a Phoenician genetic legacy, together with that of ancient Egyptians, Berbers and negroid peoples. A later addition was Semitic blood from across the Red Sea. Arab merchants had crossed to Ethiopia to buy products from the interior of Africa. Subsequently, however, they settled in the highlands and created there the Kingdom of Axum ruled by a dynasty related, according to a legend, to King Solomon and Queen Sheba. As King of Kings, or Negus, they ruled all northern Ethiopia, as we know it now, and west of that to the Blue Nile. Their trading empire extended as far as Greece and Syria and the items they dealt in belie the image that Africa was simply the source of gold, slaves and ivory. *The Periplus of the Erythrean Sea* dating to the 1st century AD describes some of the goods: ,'... undressed cloth made in Egypt for the Berbers; robes from Arsinoe; cloaks of poor quality dyed in colours; double-fringed linen mantles; many articles of flint glass and others of Murrhine, made in Diaspolis; and brass, which is used for ornaments and cut in pieces instead of coin; sheets of soft copper, used for cooking utensils and cut up for bracelets and anklets for women; iron which is made into spears used against the elephants and other wild beasts, and in their wars.'

Ideas were exchanged as well as goods. In the 4th century Christianity was brought by missionaries to Ethiopia and the Negus himself was converted, together with the nobility and subsequently a great many of the common people. During the next 10 centuries, conflict raged between the Christians of Abyssinia (as Ethiopia was then known) and the Muslims of the surrounding regions, causing the Abyssinians to turn in upon themselves and shun the rest of the world. Unified against their enemies they were born as a nation.

Out of their isolation also came a certain self-sufficiency both practical and spiritual. Even now, despite immense population growth, Ethiopia could feed her people, while the Coptic Church provides a focus badly needed among people of so many origins.

Yet the problems that face Ethiopia today underscore the inherent divisions amongst her peoples, for not only are there the age-old enmities between Arab and Christian but the territorial imperative is becoming more apparent. The province of Eritrea in the north is rallying itself against the central government, demanding independence. On a much smaller scale, the people of land traditionally held are beginning to compete with one another for the more marginal zones: the steep slopes and the arid areas that were never previously farmed. From the land they already work, they are coaxing the maximum – and more. To cook their food they have cut down the tree cover, and where land worked year after year to feed the family begins to fail under cultivation, cattle are brought in. Continuous trampling and feeding on the abused land finally strips the last vestiges of plant growth.

In the years of drought which have affected Ethiopia, particularly in the early 1970s, nature seemed to be giving warning of her displeasure. The drought itself imposed hardships and the sparse vegetation on punished land was finally destroyed and, when the rains returned, they transformed the landscape into runnelled wastelands, tearing away the fertile layer on which future harvests depended. Thus, the Ethiopian farmer is not only increasingly bereft of his soil, but also bereft of alternatives. As long as his family continues to grow and there is no longer any additional land which he can effectively utilise, he is destined to watch his fortunes decline. Under such circumstances, it is not surprising that aggression is rife in this part of the world.

Ethiopia was not the only country affected by the terrible droughts of the 1970s; northern Kenya, the Sudan – indeed the entire Sahelian fringe as far west as Mauritania – was affected. More than a quarter of a million died, and many millions more – especially children – were permanently affected. Once their plight became known, emergency supplies of food were given by various other countries, but efforts to distribute the aid were hampered by an almost total lack of transport to the affected regions and by the greed and corruption of local officials. The toll of the drought goes far beyond the immediate losses in lives and livestock: children who suffered severe malnutrition have in many cases suffered permanent brain damage or been blinded, and will in future place a further burden on the resources of these regions.

Yet in terms of human history this drought is probably not the worst experienced in the Sahel. Why then was the suffering so great and the losses so high? The Nuer, the Nuba and the Karamajong have herded their cattle here for centuries, and although the oral tradition recalls years when the rains failed, it nowhere reflects the almost total disaster that afflicts them now. The Shilluk and Masai have also known times of terrible drought in their past. Why has the aftermath of these parched years had such seemingly irrevocable effects?

The Sahel is in essence a marginal area where the total aridity of the desert begins to give way to kinder climes in which rain, although erratic and highly seasonal, maintains the hardy grasses and drought-resistant shrubs and trees such as the thorny acacias, the commiphoras, the boscias and the grewias.

If one flies south along the Great Rift Valley over the Danakil Desert towards Lake Turkana on the border between Ethiopia and Kenya, the character of the Sahel becomes apparent for it heralds the start of the savannahs. It is also the frontline of a war between the desolation of the desert and the comparative fertility of the more productive areas. At this moment, with man inadvertently aiding the enemy, the Sahara is advancing at an estimated rate of 50 kilometres a year on a broad front. It may well be that the larger forces of climatic change are at work, but by using up every scrap of vegetation, man makes the desert's victory more swift and certain.

To the east and to the west of the Rift stretch the high and largely featureless plains of the African plateau. At first they are covered by steppe vegetation – patches of grass and small low shrubs. But slowly, as one traverses the hundreds of kilometres of Africa's savannahs, the grass cover becomes fuller and more vigorous and trees appear singly, here and there. Still further south, as the rainfall increases, the grasses sweep the plains, green just after the rains, to become gradually, coarse and yellow as the dry season sets in. Here and there are clumps of trees, and along the river-courses a fringe of green; in some areas trees predominate, creating a lacework canopy over the land. In all its many guises this is the African savannah and, apart from the desert areas, the most widespread environment on the continent.

Long ago, man learnt that cattle thrive in these regions: the pastoralists of East Africa have grazed their herds here for perhaps thousands of years. Yet their recent history has not been a happy one and the droughts of the last decade have delivered a shattering blow.

Initially, when Britain colonised Kenya at the end of the 19th century, the land seemed ideal for cultivation and indeed on the highlands is to be found some of the finest agricultural land in Africa. The savannahs, however, are not nearly as productive as they seem. The soils are generally poor in organic material, nitrogen and phosphates, furthermore the better ones occur patchily which makes for difficult management. The climate is capricious as well; the rainfall varies dramatically from one year to the next, and is often late and ravaging.

The natural grasses are superbly adapted to these conditions; even after severe drought they can be counted on to come up green with the first rains. So, too are the trees adapted to these conditions, although they tend to thin out where the soil is shallow, less fertile and rainfall is scant. Only now that scientists have begun to understand the potential uses of the savannah has traditional pastoralism come into truer perspective as one of the most rewarding and secure livelihood it offers.

The Masai, like several other groups such as the Fulani of West Africa and the Dinka of the Nile Sudd, is the quintessential pastoralist whose cattle are his livelihood and his status symbol. Traditionally, they are the only tangible form of wealth he values.

None of Africa's pastoralists are 'cattle worshippers' as so often portrayed by outsiders. Yet it is difficult to find a parallel in western cultures to help explain the relationship adequately – money alone does not imbue a man with the same qualities. To the Masai his cattle also are a symbol of his material status and, by extension, the way in which others regard him. On the purely practical level, cattle provide food in the form of milk, sometimes mixed with blood – and, on special occasions, meat as well. Their hides have a multitude of uses from clothing to the covering of shields, and their horns are made into items such as containers for medicinal herbs.

The Masai used to follow migration patterns in which, after the rains, they took their herds away from the best land to the more arid areas. Here they took advantage of the new growth and, as the dry season set in, gradually retreated back to the richer pasture which they knew would last them through the long months until the following rainy season.

The European administrators chose to reallocate the Masai land in the belief that cultivation was a more worthy way of life than one of pastoralism, and so all land believed to be in any way suited to crops was awarded to farmers – most often white settlers. Since the Masai consider a sedentary life beneath their dignity, and since their best pasturage was often judged to be ideal farmland, in the subsequent allocation of land they found themselves deprived of the very areas upon which the success of their herding depended. The result has been tragic.

On the poor pasture left to them they struggle to survive as before, but without success. Only those fortunate enough to have both rainy and dry season pasture can continue with the life they know best; that of warrior pastoralists striding proudly across the plains beside their cattle. But even their future is insecure through an apparent paradox. The cattle diseases that in the past drastically reduced the herds have now been brought under control. In the short term these Masai believe that their fortunes are improving, but since they are restricted and cannot expand to areas other than the semi-desert, pressure of animals will destroy the very pasture they now enjoy. Some marry women from cultivator tribes such as the Kikuyu so that crops will augment their diet, but for many the only alternative is to leave and drift, apathetic and destitute, to the towns in the hope of making a living as unskilled workers.

Ironically, the efficient ways of the Masai pastoralists have received belated recognition. On some of what was once their land, given to white farmers, it was found that cultivation could not be sustained and that commercial ranching was a better proposition. Yet the ranchers were disappointed to find that where the Masai herds had fattened and multiplied theirs did not, even on this the best of the pastoralists' land. Faced with the expense of buying silage and the evident failure of their methods, they called in researchers to make an assessment. Their recommendation was unequivocal: if the ranches were to be self-sustaining, the owners should offer to purchase from the Masai the dry pastures they still held and follow the same grazing methods as the traditional pastoralist. But while this may solve the problems of commercial ranchers it has done little to solve the dilemmas of the Masai – and shared by all the traditional pastoralists of Africa. Not only have they been dismissed in favour of people who till the soil, but they have been pushed into more and more marginal areas as the demands of a rapidly growing population bring more of their land under the plough.

This vicious cycle brings us back to the questions raised by the Sahelian disasters, for today the pastoralists have little option but to live there or accept drastic changes to the fabric of their lives. Deprived of the alternative of a retreat to lusher areas in time of drought, and prevented by law from raiding cattle, they take a fatalistic view. Yet they maintain their cultural values according to which the size of a man's herd is more important than its condition while their environment is rapidly degenerating under the pressures exerted on it by the cattle themselves, the constant search for firewood and, above all, the recent failures of the rains.

In a sense the traditional pastoralists are in a cultural cul-de-sac and although their past identity has been linked totally to this way of life, their future survival as a people must allow for fundamental cultural change. The environment has made this clear, for as one researcher pointed out, in these arid zones 'the alternative is no longer between pastoral nomadism and agriculture, but between pastoral nomadism and nothing'.

The loss of life in the Sahel is testimony to the predictions of the Club of Rome's project on the predicament of mankind. On the basis of mathematical models they have shown that 'the basic behaviour mode of the world system is exponential growth of population and capital followed by collapse'. In the case of the Sahelian regions, cattle are the capital and their numbers have increased essentially as a result of veterinary technology. The human numbers grew too, and this can be explained partly in terms of natural increase, and also partly because of innoculation against disease, and some degree of health care.

The Sahel by its very nature is an area of limited productivity and serves well to illustrate the plight of man in an environment pushed close to its upper limit by his need to survive. The drought triggered the 'overshoot and collapse' principle. With the environment unquestionably unable to sustain the population, malnutrition and its attendant miseries set in. People died not so much from the lack of food but from the diseases that cut them down ruthlessly now that they were so weakened. The same applies to the cattle and livestock.

Given the short time in which the people of Africa are doubling in number (approximately 30 years at present) and the limits of resources such as land and water, this same tragedy may well be repeated again and again as more of the continent reaches a critically marginal state.

Population pressure has also affected that singularly African phenomenon, the wildlife of the savannahs. Nowhere else in the natural world has there ever been the sheer mass of animal life found here, nor the diversity of mammals. The explanation lies in the diversity of the grasses themselves. They blanket great tracts of Africa's tropical regions with a plethora of species of different heights and different compositions according to the particular environment.

Fire has been a major creative force in the savannahs, for towards the end of the dry season, the land is parched, the vegetation dry and inflammable. Before man came, the lightning heralding the coming rains was the primary cause of the fires that annually consume and help to recycle as much as a quarter of the grasslands. Sometimes the flames sweep across the land ahead of the driving winds, casting smoke into the skies; at other times the fire works slowly forward, its intense heat damaging the vegetation even more seriously. And when the flames are gone, the landscape is charred and seemingly dead. Yet, at the

133

first approach of rain, the grass almost miraculously puts up its sweet young shoots from the still living roots.

But the trees do not recover so speedily although some species have become fire-resistant to a degree. Particularly when subjected to a slow burn, the bark and trunk are scorched, and below the heated soil the roots are damaged too. Young trees often do not survive.

For at least 6 000 years men in Africa have also played a part in the formation of grassland. They knew that fresh new growth springs from the ashes of natural fires, and went about inducing these conditions.

Just before the rains, they set the grass alight; the fires race uncontrolled across the land and, since rain may still be weeks away, their effect is dramatic. Huge swathes of African savannah are blackened, the panicking game herds left in disarray, twitching and nervous along its boundaries.

Later, when the people became cultivators, they cleared the bush and trees to make their fields, usually burning back the vegetation in the process. And above all they chopped trees for firewood and to build their huts. All along trees were felled, burnt and inhibited so that grasses came eventually to dominate.

The African herbivores have also played a part in the spread of grassland at the expense of trees. Not only do their feeding habits encourage the spread of certain grasses and inhibit others, but by feeding from the crowns of saplings, the browsers such as giraffe and eland, kudu and gerenuk encourage bushy growth rather than the development of tall trees. Cattle increase these pressures, keeping the grasses cropped and, simultaneously, manured.

Recently a fascinating interaction between the impala and the *Acacia tortilis* was discovered, illustrating something of the complexity of the relationship between all living things. The impala is extremely fond of the seed pods of this particular tree and while the advantages to the impala were obvious, no one suspected that this was part of a two-way relationship. The seeds pass through the antelope's system and on the way its gastric juices soften the outer covering of the seed. This too is not surprising. However, it has been proven that *Acacia tortilis* seeds simply left in the soil fail to germinate and that passage through the impala's digestive tract is vital for germination.

No doubt there are many more such links in the intricate savannah ecosystems and slowly, as we begin to gain a fuller understanding of their complexities, we can apply this knowledge to the better management not only of Africa's wildlife reserves but to the landscape of the continent as a whole.

Wise land use is the key to sustainability – to the ways in which to develop areas so that their productivity is retained as easily and as naturally as possible. Here the scientist is at work, analysing slowly and carefully the many interdependent factors of which soil and climate are but two; unravelling the mysteries of the ecosystems so that they can be used and not abused. The price of abuse is already frighteningly evident wherever man in Africa has sought to win more from the earth without at the same time in any way restraining his population growth and his seemingly endless desire for material wealth. Against this background of greed and self-interest, the survival of Africa's natural heritage is under severe pressure, even in the very areas set aside for its preservation.

Good management of these reserves is a highly controversial subject, for so often it requires actions which are construed by some as contrary to the spirit of conservation. Yet Africa's wildlife, if it is to survive at all, needs to be managed with both ecological and economic objectives in mind. Researcher John Hanks says: 'Aesthetic and cultural factors are important but . . . economic and ecological considerations alone will determine the survival of many of the wildlife areas. Food and economics have high priority so that if wildlife populations can produce worthwhile quantities of protein and earn foreign exchange on a sustained yield basis, an economic justification for conservation is likely to gain wide support.'

To the peasant farmer already suffering the effects of too little land to which to apply his traditional shifting cultivation, the wildlife reserves appear to be a blatant waste of land. He sees his future survival blocked by laws and regulations that seem to give priority to giraffe rather than people.

Africa cannot afford wildlife reserves as a 'luxury'; they must be shown to be a necessity – and economically viable. Only education will help the peasant farmer, casting a covetous eye at the reserves, to change his views; firstly by providing him with the skills and technology to make his own

land self-sustaining, and secondly by equipping him with a better grasp of the workings of national wealth so that he comes to realise that the reserves can benefit him through earning revenues for health care and education, sanitation and public transport.

But many do not wait for the central governments to disburse the earnings from tourism and the sale of meat, horn and hides of culled animals. They take their profits directly and with ruthless efficiency. Almost daily the poacher is at work with silent traps in the wildlife reserves. His prime targets are elephant ivory and rhinoceros horn. The animals are killed, the ivory or horn hacked out there and then, and the carcasses left abandoned. Nature's scavengers – hyaena, jackal, vulture and marabou among others – attend the feast but often the carnage is too great even for their appetites and the carcasses eventually rot.

Rhinoceros have been entirely wiped out in many parts because customers, particularly in the East, quite mistakenly believe that the powdered horn has aphrodisiac qualities. Ivory has been in vogue since Pharaonic times and down the centuries its popularity has remained high. The elephants of West Africa were decimated and East and southern Africa's great pachyderms were hunted and harried, for there is no way to obtain the great curving tusks except by killing the animal first. Researcher John Tinker reported in 1975 that an estimated 10 000 to 20 000 elephant were being killed each year in Kenya alone.

When wildlife reserves were set aside to conserve Africa's rapidly dwindling fauna and flora, the elephants' fortunes took a turn for the better. This great beast has no real enemies except man and now, within the wildlife reserves where man's depredations are severely curtailed, its situation has changed. In the very areas set aside for its conservation, the elephant has become in the opinion of many concerned and responsible people, a destructive force.

In keeping with his size an adult male elephant does not only have a gargantuan appetite, but in pursuit of his daily diet he damages and seemingly wastes his habitat. He will nudge over a fully grown tree for a few pods at the crown, or strip great mouthfuls of bark leaving mature trees vulnerable to insects and disease.

To watch a herd during its 18 hours or more of feeding is to understand the concerns of the protagonists of culling. Without doubt the large populations of elephant confined to the reserves are increasing to the point where their profligate feeding habits are entirely changing the habitat and therefore threatening not only themselves but the lives of the many other creatures that share it.

While the 'cull or not to cull' argument dickers hotly back and forth, many reserves have begun to cull not only the elephant but also the rapidly growing herds of antelope. The meat is then sold either dried and salted or frozen to the protein-starved markets in towns and villages. Wild meat is a highly marketable commodity and the process of culling therefore benefits both the reserves and the population at large.

The need to cull at all arises from the reality that conservation areas specially set aside are rarely large enough to allow the natural checks and balances of the ecosystem to function adequately.

All along the Great Rift Valley the alkaline lakes provide outstanding examples of still functioning ecosystems, each with a character of its own. The alkaline content of the volcanic spills in the Rift makes their water sodary and bitter; other lakes along the Rift, however, are clear and deep. Lake Tanzania, second in depth only to Lake Baikal in Russia, is like a limpid inland sea, rich in fish such as the massive Nile perch. Others like Lake Natron are lurid with algae that bloom in waters so rich in bicarbonate of soda that soda-rimmed pockmarks stipple the surface.

The soda lakes are the haunt of the flamingo and over three million of them travel the Rift to feed on the algae-rich waters. Pelicans, too, nest on the soda flats, safe from all but the most determined land predators. Nobody wants the soda lakes which have consequently retained their strange and pristine beauty. But the clear sweet lakes have great economic potential and attract man: he harvests the fish, uses the lakes to travel from place to place along its shores, and increasingly and heedlessly casts his wastes there.

The lakes are particularly characteristic of the Eastern and highly fragmented arm of the Rift Valley, which splits into two separate systems in the region north of Lake Victoria. Here are some of the most over-taxed areas in Africa.

Rwanda is the most densely populated area on the continent, with an average density of 140 peo-

**117, 118, 119, 120** It is difficult for the Western mind to conceive of sophisticated artistic expression among peoples of limited technological achievement. Yet in southern Sudan live the Nuba who, in their face and body painting, express a harmony and an aesthetic appreciation of line and form evocative of Picasso's finest work.

Nuban body art reveals a visual sophistication based on a keen appreciation of the human form and of the world in which it functions. For a woman, from puberty until she bears her first child, this entails scarification which leaves her torso densely marked with neat rows of tiny raised welts and dots; some are just to enhance her charms, others are proud symbols of her fertility and womanhood.

Marriageable men paint their faces and decorate their bodies with ochres, red haematite and, more recently, blue tints introduced by the Arabs. Peering intently into small mirrors, they embellish their bodies with abstract and representational designs. Since the Nuba bathe daily, the paintings are constantly being changed, and although some exponents are clearly better than others, the overall level of artistic expression is refined.

Particularly after the harvest, the Nuba indulge in art and love. The young people dust themselves with ochre (117) and anoint their skin with sesame oil so that they gleam sinuously. Hair is shaven into the distinctive style and dressed (118). Then comes the dance of love. While the eligible youths sit, eyes downcast (120), the girls dance closer and closer (119) until they choose their man – sometimes for a night, sometimes for life.

**121** As if carved from obsidian, a naked Nuba drives his riding ox past the pink and gray granite of his mountain home. His companion wears clothes, for the Nuba cover the body if misshapen, sickly or beyond its youthful prime.

**122** Sorghum cascades into a typical Nuban granary for storage through the long, dry months ahead. The Nuba traditionally build their homesteads on hillsides, perching them naturally on and around boulders so that the huts seem to sprout from the earth from which they are made.

Nuban architecture is beautifully conceived and economically constructed both in terms of human effort and in the use of local materials: rocks and stones for dry foundations, long sapling-thick timbers for the framework, mud for the walls and cool thatch for the roof. Granaries and huts are narrow and tubular. The entrances to the granaries and to the special bad-weather sleeping quarters are about two metres above the ground through a circular opening little more than the width of a man's hips. With the fluid grace born of practice, the Nuba twist and flick their bodies through the aperture to the dry cool interior, safe from snakes, scorpions and rodents.

Today the Nuban dwelling is essentially a shelter from the sun that can push shade temperatures to well over 40 °C day after day, and from the savage downpours of the rainy season. From the outside, however, there is an undeniably fortress-like quality to the homesteads and indeed this factor was once important. The Nuba claim that their mountain villages kept them safe from Arab slave traders and, later, from British colonial rule. But highland villages offer other advantages too: the rain runs off quickly, skirting the specially-raised floors of the huts and mountain shadows alleviate the summer heat.

**123** The Nuba are starting to venture from the mountains onto the plains, attracted by foreign goods and modern lifestyles, so beginning to lose their own distinctive identity. It may well be that within a generation from now the only face painting to be found here will be that produced for tourists.

*Following page* (124): Sandstone and sun in Ethiopia's hellish-hot Danakil Depression where some of the highest temperatures on earth have been recorded. It is possible to fry an egg without using anything other than the unrelenting sun.

121 122
123

*Previous page* (125): English historian Edward Gibbon aptly observed of Ethiopia in the 18th century: 'Encompassed on all sides by enemies of their religion, the Aethiopians slept near a thousand years, forgetful of the world by whom they were forgotten.' This isolation born of religious conflict accounts for Ethiopia's distinctive culture which is of Africa and yet not African. At Lalibala, this rock-hewn church emphasises the inherent introversion that pervades Ethiopian history and the rôle of her Christian churches which gave both cohesion and identity to her peoples.

**126, 127** More than 4 000 of Ethiopia's many churches are carved into the very mountains themselves. Access to these unique hiding-places is often along difficult paths but the reward lies in the dimly-lit interiors with their rich legacy of religious frescoes. Often the precise derivation of these exuberant works of art is lost in the amalgam of styles and symbols evolved over more than 1 500 years during which the churches employed foreign artists and craftsmen. It is known that in the 17th century Indian craftsmen were brought here and one senses the imprint of their culture in some of the wall paintings (126). Byzantine and 15th century Venetian artists have also left their subtle mark (127).

**128** On his island retreat on Lake Haik, the Bishop of this Coptic monastery reads the original Amharic version of the Bible.

146

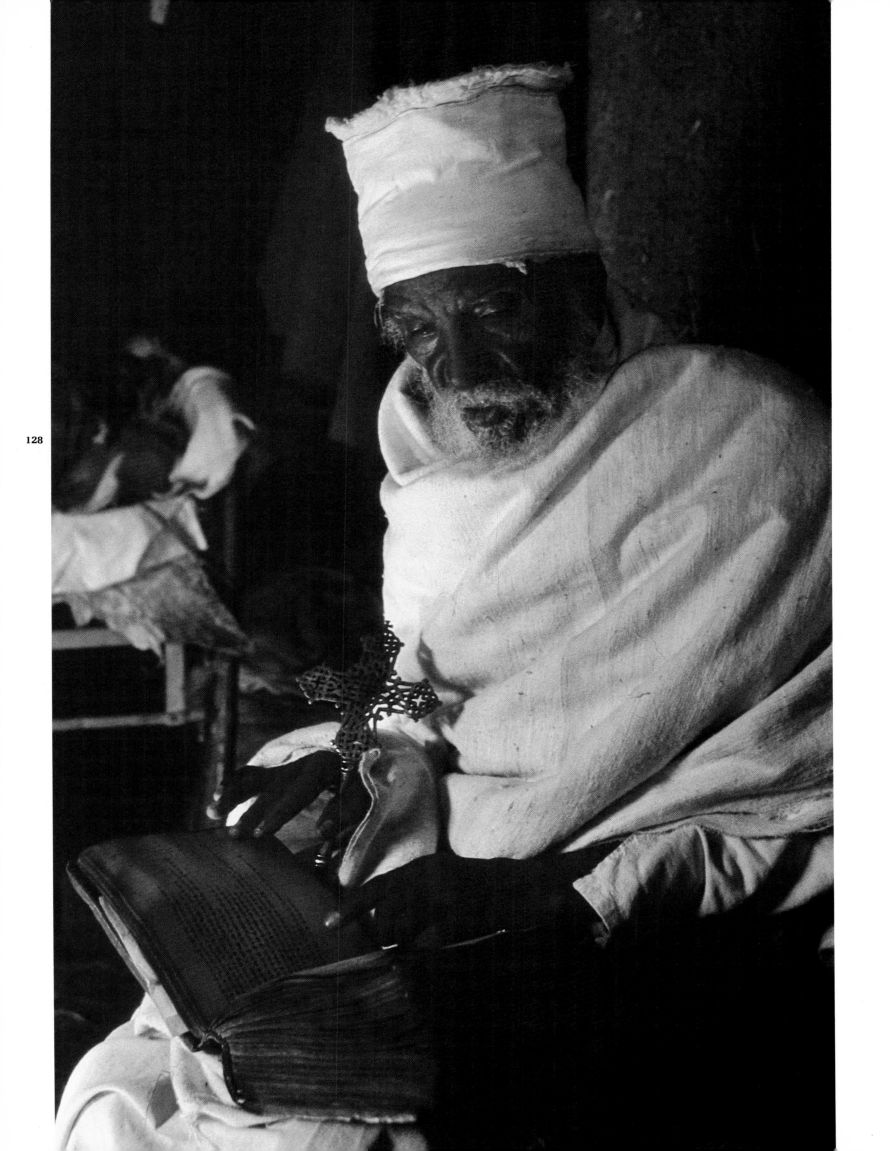

**129** Today he works for the railway, but in his fierce eyes glimmers the independent spirit of Ethiopian warriors of the past. This fighting spirit is still strong among his people and inflames the unresolved conflicts that make the horn of Africa unsettled and volatile.

**130** At this Afar encampment, barren earth and acacia brush fences are evidence of the burden man and his herds place on marginal lands. The Danakil Desert is one of the most unrelenting areas in Africa; achingly dry for almost nine months of the year, hot and tediously flat, it stretches from the Ethiopian escarpment to the Red Sea.

That the Afar tribesmen live here is a tribute to man's capacity to adapt; but that their population has reached 250 000 is the basis of their tragedy. By keeping on the move with their herds of camels, cattle and goats, they

**130**

131

have eked out a living, but they are fast outstripping the desert's ability to sustain them. Pressed by their increasing numbers to return to areas which have not yet recovered from earlier visits, they hasten the forces which degrade the land. Stripped first of acacia trees and then by erosion, the Danakil is being destroyed by the very people whose survival depends on its favours.

**131** Sloe-eyed and as delicately drawn as an Egyptian princess on a Theban frieze, an Ethiopian maiden reflects her singular ancestry – part Semite, part Hamite. Her semitic ancestors crossed the Red Sea from Arabia, whence the influence of Sheba, whose beauty was also legend, reached out to Africa.

*Following page* (132): On the edges of Lake Abbé in Djibouti, strange bicarbonate spires mark springs rising to the surface.

149

*Previous page* (133): Fires of cattle dung cast a dense pall over Dinka herdsmen and their cattle, protecting them from the tireless assaults of mosquitoes. Here, in their homeland close to the source of the Nile, the Dinka also coat themselves with the ash from these pungent fires as a precaution.

The Dinka epitomise the traditional pastoralist of the African savannah to whom cattle represent the ultimate both in status and in wealth. Basil Davidson makes the point: 'The Dinka have become obsessed by cattle as the modern man has by money, and for comparable reasons. The one, like the other, confers status as well as a livelihood.' Their beasts are in themselves of little merit as beef stock for they tend to be small, compact and wiry; at first glance, their only feature worthy of note is their heroically proportioned horns. But one cannot judge these cattle by such criteria, for the Dinka do not intend them primarily for food but as a store of wealth and to this end have selectively bred specimens that are instead long-lived and resistant to disease.

The Dinka's commitment to his cattle is no irrational obsession. Seen in the context of the sweeping savannah grasslands, the virtues of his choice of currency are self-evident. Away from the river pastures, on higher ground, the Dinka build permanent villages and here they raise crops, but the soils are so poor that they find little reward for their efforts. At best a man grows enough to keep the porridge pot filled year round. But if the savannah soils yield little more than a minimal harvest, its grasslands ensure that his cattle increase and flourish.

**134** For this Dinka child drinking milk from a calabash in his father's cattle camp, the pastoralist way of life may be coming to an end. As long as they can remember, the Dinka have been moving with their herds from the swamps of the Nile Sudd to dry land and back again.

**135** On a hunt in the papyrus swamps of the Nile Sudd, Dinka pole their canoe through shallows haunted by the elusive Nile lechwe.

134

**136** Sweeping points of light trace the passage of flamingos scrambling into the air over Lake Nakuru – rendezvous of Africa's three million flame-pink flamingos, and site of one of the greatest wildlife spectacles in the world.

Nakuru is just one of several warm caustic lakes scattered along Africa's Great Rift Valley. The concentration of sodium carbonate, or soda, in the lakes varies from the hellhole conditions of Lake Magadi where almost no living thing can survive, to Lake Nakuru whose bitter, alkaline-rich waters create a habitat for the organisms adapted to its peculiar conditions.

These soda lakes provide a tempting mass of potential food in the form of algae, small shrimplike animals and various tiny snails, in an environment which makes it inaccessible to most creatures. Yet somewhere in its evolution, the flamingo took advantage of this lavish food supply and in the process had to make the critical change from opportunist to specialist; for to feed here requires adaptations that have tied the flamingo inexorably to a very particular mode of life.

Of the many adaptations this entailed, the flamingo's beak must be its notable achievement, for it separates the minute organisms on which the bird lives from the deadly soup in which they occur. Yet there are dangers in such specialisation, for such a highly developed beak cannot cope with a sudden change of diet. Therefore inherent in the flamingo's success is the factor that it has become adapted to a habitat that is both sufficiently widespread and constantly fruitful.

But a new and ominous influence is intruding on this balance. Close to the lake, the town of Nakuru boasts a population of well over 60 000 people whose effluent is gradually polluting the waters of the lake, leaving the flamingo trapped in a habitat man now threatens to destroy.

**137-141** When in the 1960s naturalist John Hillaby visited the El Molo on Lake Turkana's bleak shores, 'the impression,' he said, 'was neolithic.' Impoverished and crippled by disease, there were then fewer than 300 El Molo left, clinging to the only life they knew, and to the lake that is their life.

Out on the dull blue-green surface of the alkaline lake, the El Molo come into their own: skilfully guiding their simple doum palm rafts, they hunt the great Nile perch, which can grow here to 90 kilograms or more, and the crocodile.

The crocodiles, like the people, are small and often hungry. There are an estimated 12 000 competing with one another – and with man – for Lake Turkana's fish. For some unknown reason they seem to feed mainly on the bream, a mere morsel next to the Nile perch and this

scanty diet combined with the pressures of competition may well account for their stunted growth.

Commercial hunters spurned them because their skins were thickly calloused – possibly as a result of their alkaline habitat – but to the El Molo, their odoriferous flesh is a delicacy.

Balancing on his raft, an El Molo fisherman unerringly plunges his harpoon into a crocodile lurking well below the surface (137), and after a brief tussle the 1,70 metre saurian is hauled aboard (138). The catch is carried back to the homestead (139) where the children keenly watch it being gutted and skinned (140), for roasted over the open fire it will make the evening meal. What cannot be eaten today will be dried for tomorrow. Beyond the cooking fire the setting sun tints lake and sky with soft hues, and soon darkness will envelop the El Molo (141).

**137    138**

**142** To relate the prehistory of Africa is to relate the prehistory of mankind, and the unique environment of the Great Rift Valley has proved to be a singular custodian of this past. In the Olduvai gorge, and at a dozen other sites in this great north-south gash in the face of Africa, archaeologists have been tentatively piecing together the story of the origins of man. There are great gaps in their knowledge, and work is painstakingly slow for in the 100 metres of layered sediments exposed by erosion at Olduvai alone is a record of two million years of human prehistory.

Key figure in the long and successful line of hominids we acknowledge as our ancestors is a small somewhat ape-like creature known as *Ramapithecus.* The events that placed him in the wings of an African setting are at once fortuitous and intriguing. About twelve million years ago the world was far warmer and wetter than today and *Ramapithecus* was, in a sense, a 'man of the world' for he was scattered widely in his tropical forest habitat not only in Africa but as far north as modern Germany and in the great verdant stretches across Asia to China and beyond. But he had not ventured into the New World of the Americas when the earth climate began to change, becoming progressively cooler and drier until it was only in Africa that there existed remnant tropical forest with *Ramapithecus* still in residence. What happened to his German or Chinese cousins is at this point irrelevant for they were not fated to survive the changes to their environment or to make the crucial adaptations that would lead to the evolution of man.

But he was not the only primate in the forest, and as it continued to shrink, so competition between the various ape-like species must have become ever more intense. This was probably the single most important factor that impelled *Ramapithecus* to make the crucial change from forest-dweller to a life on the African savannah. He found himself in a unique position: although his tropical home had shrunk drastically and his leafy canopy was thinning out, an alternative presented itself in the tall grasses and scattered trees of the true African savannah.

It is unlikely that he then turned his back on his former arboreal home and marched off onto the grassy plains; successful adaptation to a new environment is generally the result of lengthy trial and error. But at a certain point in his forays to the ground *Ramapithecus* crossed the threshold to this new world, in the process closing the door to his past. Never again could he return to the safety of the branches: he was irrevocably set on the incredible journey that would lead from ape-man to man-ape and, finally, to man himself.

*Following page* (143): Typically Africa: acacias, wildebeest and a fierce sun veiled by dust.

**144** With quick, deft movements a Rendille woman prepares twine for cattle halters.

**145** A Rendille woman wears as jewellery cowrie shells on a leather strap slung over her shoulder.

**146** Reminiscent of America's dustbowls, such hostile scenery is becoming more and more commonplace in East Africa. And, invariably, commanding centre stage in the scenario is the goat.

Wherever the savannah has deteriorated under the combined pressures of man and herds, the goat is brought in to devour the final scraps, for this remarkable creature is the complete opportunist of the herbivorous world. Its talent lies in finding sustenance from the most meagre and unpromising sources. On this scanty diet it produces a surprising quantity of milk, and provides meat, leather and hair for weaving. Thus, for many of Africa's savannah dwellers forced by population pressure to live in marginal areas, the goat is often the last and only means of survival. But once a herd of goats has stripped the land, no scrap of green remains.

The solution contains a tragic paradox, for to ban the goats from these regions would be inhuman while man still struggles to live there.

*Following page* (147): North of Nairobi, Samburu youths in full regalia attend an initiation dance.

**148, 149, 150** Sensing danger, this buffalo takes a bold and aggressive stance, his lethal horns making an impressive display. Buffaloes in their prime have few enemies other than man, but once age has slowed and weakened them, lion take their opportunity. Under moonlight the pride attacks and after a brief, powerful tussle, one of the lionesses delivers the *coup de grâce*.

By midday, the pride has taken its fill and has left the remains of the feast to the scavengers. There is indeed a certain beauty in the order in which the scavengers arrive, their various assaults on the carcass and the efficiency with which they dispose of the buffalo in less than 36 hours. The spotted hyaenas (149) get in first to bite and tear at the carcass, crunching even the bones between their massive molars; unattractive as they are, they act as highly effective scavengers.

With the rising sun, the vultures begin to arrive, species by species, each with its preferences, each with its particular scavenging talents. Most numerous are the white-backed (150), squabbling here for a choice bit of entrail and a place at the carcass. Later still, when the vultures have picked most of the meat from the bones, the jackals, as well as other birds and insects, come for the leftovers. Finally, microbes take over and within days nothing remains but the great bossed horns.

**151** Removed from bothersome insects, a male lion enjoys the cooling breeze in a tall tree in the Manyara National Park, Tanzania.

*Following page* (152): A mass of wildebeest on the move return to Serengeti's freshly greened plains.

But it is not only these teeming numbers that make Africa's savannah unique. Equally remarkable is the diversity of animals it sustains: the secret lies in the wealth of grasses, herbs, shrubs and trees which create a natural pasture of unparalleled richness – a result of soil and sunlight, fire and drought which, together, have brought forth an environment relatively poor in trees but rich in grasses.

Each species of antelope has behavioural and anatomical adaptations to the particular savannah habitat it has made its own. But all along there is interaction, and overlap in feeding between the different species. On Serengeti's plains wildebeest, zebra and Thomson's gazelle share the green repast. Yet they are not competing for the grasses. Each one is a selective feeder: the zebra eat the taller, tougher growth, wildebeest choose the somewhat shorter, leafier cover, while Thomson's gazelle nip the sweet new shoots.

Between November and May thousands upon thousands of animals are scattered across the plain and Serengeti's lions are satisfied and well-fed. Gradually, however, the grass is cropped down, and new shoots will not appear until the following rains. First to leave for other pastures are the zebra seeking more nutritious fare in Western Serengeti with its higher rainfall and better soils. Towards the end of May the wildebeest follow, leaving Thomson's gazelle to take the last of the green and nibble at the shrubs.

Five months later the dry season is at its peak; it is hot and desperately dry and all three species have removed the last shreds of sustenance from Northern Serengeti. The herds are lean and impatient. Many of the females are heavy with calf and hungry. And then, without discernible reason or warning, begins the great return. Do they smell the distant rain or does some genetic imprint drive them south? No one knows. But bucking and kicking with excitement, the wildebeest complete the final lap of their annual 500 kilometre migration.

**153** Reaching for a meal, the gerenuk stands poised on muscular hind legs, its elongated neck outstretched. Rather than compete for the already heavily grazed grasses this antelope has taken to the shrubs, using its narrow mouth and mobile lips to pluck tiny nutritious buds and leaves from between the thorns.

**154** For the Thomson's gazelle there is safety in numbers: many eyes to keep watch for approaching predators, and better odds against being the individual chosen as prey.

**155** Early in the morning, a family of cheetah come down to the watering hole. These sleek cats, known for their speed, hunt by the

chase but often lose their kills to the bigger predators such as lion and the more aggressive ones such as hyaena and wild dog. Indeed where lions are killed off by farmers, the cheetahs are able to come into their own and they flourish.

*Following page* (156): In the Far East the demand for rhino horn is all but insatiable and poachers have pursued these animals almost to extinction. The rhino's horn is not horn at all but an accretion of long hairs and even as it is not what it seems, so its aphrodisiac qualities are entirely unfounded. Perhaps this normally sluggish creature's half-hour-long sexual exertions account for the myth.

**163** A Masai *moran,* magnificently ochred and coifed, casts an experienced eye over his herds grazing in the shadow of Mount Meru. Like the Dinka, the Fulani, the Zulu – indeed like so many of the traditional pastoralists of the African savannah – the Masai is finely attuned to the land: he knows its seasons and its soils, its grasses and their uses.

Only recently have outsiders begun to appreciate the sophistication and wisdom of Masai land use, but as has so often been the case in Africa, insight has come only after much damage has been done. The ecological acumen of the Masai is revealed in their traditional cycle that began with the rainy season when they moved their herds to the more arid areas, to take advantage of the fragile new growth there. As the dry season set in, they then slowly led their cattle towards the more generous areas where the grass could be counted on to provide grazing until the start of another cycle.

But to many of the economic and development advisers and administrators who came to Africa, the Masai must have seemed feckless and wasteful, moving their herds in leisurely fashion from pasture to pasture without profit or surplus. Sincerely believing that a sedentary life as a cultivator was more worthy than a nomadic pastoral one, they allocated much of the Masai's dry season pasturage to farmers and, later, expelled them from the great plains such as Serengeti.

The Masai now found themselves deprived of half the land on which their cycle was based; they could either continue as before on the remaining land, or give up their nomadic lifestyle and settle down either as farmers in their own right or as workers.

Those who still had both wet and dry pastures, maintained their old ways, but most were less fortunate. Initially they tried to make do, but by using the same land year round, the cattle soon grazed it down to bare earth and left an eroded, sterile landscape. Bereft of their wealth in cattle, many of these Masai, stricken and apathetic, have drifted into the towns.

There can be no doubt that their traditional way of life is coming to an end and it would be foolish to suggest that a pastoral existence on the slopes of Mount Meru is an ideal to which all should aspire. Yet in their self-sustaining use of the environment, the Masai pastoralists embodied values which could serve as a model for a developed world heedlessly plundering natural resources at a frightening and progressive rate.

**164** Each gleaming and redolent with butter mixed with ochre, a Masai mother bejewels her daughter on the morning of the wedding celebrations.

**165, 166** Apprentice Morans at a ceremony (166) in their honour are blessed with a spray of milk (165).

164

165  166

**167** To the accompaniment of drums, a Giriama horn-player blasts resonant tones from this traditional instrument.

**168** In its heyday during the 18th and 19th centuries the town of Lamu on Kenya's northern coast was a bustling entrepôt in the long established trade between Asia and Africa. Today, peaceful if slightly shabby, the town's winding narrow streets recall the more prosperous past when the Arab dhows came to trade finely worked daggers and hatchets, glass vessels, wheat and crisp cotton cloth, for African ivory and slaves, tortoise shell and rhino horn.

Often overlooked in accounts of the Asia-Africa link but extremely significant were the tropical food plants introduced from the East. Bananas and yams took easily and well in East Africa and subsequently spread from here across the continent to West Africa. Both crops provide a nutritious, abundant staple food and it has been suggested that the introduction of the banana may have helped nurture the population explosion of the Bantu-speaking peoples in Central Africa who later dispersed throughout the African subcontinent.

The towns that developed along the East Coast itself were sustained in large part by these new foods, for the cereals which are associated with urban growth elsewhere in Africa took poorly to the hot, damp conditions.

169

**169** The captain and his crew check their course. Early in 1973, the dhow *Mihandust* – literally 'I seek my homeland' – set out from Arabia to Africa, carried swiftly and unerringly by the north-east monsoon winds.

**170** Seated on Persian carpets they hope to sell, along with heavily-carved Arabian chests at the East African ports, the captain and mate keep watch.

**171** At Mombasa there are keen buyers for the cargo but increased bureaucracy, new import and export taxes and currency regulations introduce an alien note to the transactions.

When the south-west monsoon signalled the time for the return trip, the only commodity worth carrying back to Arabia was mangrove poles. The homeward journey was slow and difficult – even with the assistance of a diesel engine – and for the *Mihandust* it was her last Africa-bound journey.

**172** Poised in the *zuli* – the traditional 'heads' slung from ropes aft of the big dhows – an Iranian seaman hauls tunny aboard. Most of the fish caught en route are cleaned and packed in salt for sale later, but some are eaten by the crew to relieve the monotonous diet at sea.

**173** After more than 2 000 years of profit and adventure, the dhow trade is drawing to an end.

170

171

172

*Previous page* (174): Clustered in panic around the matriarch, elephant cows and their young trample Serengeti's verdant plain.

**175** Almost a decade after devastating drought in Tanzania's Tsavo East, the effects of its death grip are still apparent. Here in 1970-1971 almost 6 000 elephant died of starvation and thirst. Except at the hand of poachers, it is seldom that the African elephant suffers such a blow, indeed the current dilemma arises from its unrestricted population growth and the troubling question is whether or not to cull them. John Hanks explains: 'To put it in very simple terms,' he says, 'the elephants are being killed because their prolific, extravagant and wasteful feeding habits are causing spectacular changes in the vegetation.'

The damage is both well-chronicled and self-evident: the elephant is clearly destroying the very areas set aside for its continued survival, and in drastically modifying its own habitat is threatening the existence of other creatures as well.

Concerned and responsible people argue the matter and their conclusions tend to fall into one of two camps: those who believe that the elephant must be carefully culled before the damage it does is irreversible; others who claim that nature should be allowed to run her course. Probably the best approach encompasses something of both viewpoints, for, given time, nature promises to make some salutary adjustments.

It has been found, for instance, that the elephant, under pressure of increased population, displays an amazing in-built birth control system in which the females tend to begin breeding at a later age than before and bring their single calves into the world at more widely spaced intervals. But in an animal that can, and in the safety of a wildlife reserve often does, live to 60, it will take time before these remarkable natural adjustments have any real effect on current numbers. It can therefore usefully be argued that while nature slowly adapts, some elephant should be culled, thereby protecting the environment in the interim.

**176** Outspread ears exaggerating its already formidable bulk, an East African bull elephant weighing over 5 000 kilograms charges the camera in an attack that is more bluff than serious.

175    176

**177** Mist and mystery and strange giant plants cloak the high secret valleys of the Mountains of the Moon. The Swedish botanist, Hedberg, described these regions as having 'winter every night and summer every day'. To cope with such exacting conditions, the plants have undergone numerous adaptations; for example the long 'ostrich plume' lobelia visible here, flaunts a feathery coating to the elongated flower heads. Other plants have other means of protecting themselves from the daily fluctuations of temperature: some have leafy rosettes to protect the growing tips, others thick cork girdles about the stem, and hairy or waxy leaves for added insulation. Presumably gigantism is in itself an adaptation, but as yet the phenomenon is only partly understood.

**178** In 1885 Count Samuel Teleki laboured through mist and chill to become the first white man to reach the alpine zone of Mount Kenya.

as need arose. Thus the concept of private property never hindered the movement of the Bantu-speakers.

The immense importance of cattle was another feature common to them all: they represented both material wealth and the status of the male within the community. And just as the prudent man in a cash economy does not squander his money but invests it to augment his capital and provide him with financial security, so the Bantu-speaker does not eat his cattle. He devotes himself to their well-being so that he, too, may see his capital increase and his status grow. In order to subsist, however, he looks to the land.

The continent is vast, indeed, but its soils are generally extremely poor, and in the past foreigners have tended to mistake its size for its potential, and its well-developed natural plant cover for inherent productivity. The researcher W. Allan pointed out that as much as 57 per cent of the land surface was either so poor – or afflicted with so hostile a climate – that it was totally unsuited to agriculture, and a further 32 per cent consisted of poor and weak agricultural soil. He estimated that a mere 3 per cent was truly fertile and did not require lengthy fallows to remain productive.

The black farmer did not possess the scientific knowledge to prove this point, but he was fully aware of the low productivity of the soil he worked, and he knew that it could not sustain him for more than a few years at a time. This reality impelled him to move constantly, to clear new land when what he had already cultivated for a few years ceased to produce enough to feed his family.

The African cultivators were aware of the benefits of manuring and the way in which wood ash could prolong the fertility of the land. To clear the fields they would set fire to the savannah and woodland and the women with their hoes dug in the ashes before planting crops. Around the homesteads vegetables were grown to provide the 'relish' which accompanied the starch staples such as millet or maize, usually served as a thick porridge. Milk, soured with various agents, added protein to the diet, and on ceremonial occasions, an ox would be slaughtered as part of the feast.

Traditional society among the Bantu-speaking peoples reflects how closely cultural and environmental realities are linked. Normally, a homestead consisted of a man and his wife – a chief or extremely wealthy individual might have two or more wives – and their children. The homesteads, arranged loosely about the cattle kraal, belonged to people related by birth or marriage and bound together by a well-defined web of obligations and duties which, at certain times of the year, helped compensate for the shortage of labour in the individual homesteads. In Zambia, Bemba men still gather to help one another to chop down the bush and trees on land readied for planting, and also to drag vegetation from the surrounding land so that it will increase the ash once the field is burnt.

When the heads of millet or cobs of maize are heavy and ripe, large crowds of people related as much by blood as by their obligation to help one another, work side by side. And when the fields of one homestead are clear, they move together to the next, toiling from dawn to dusk under the relentless sun, stopping now and then to refresh themselves with homemade beer and savour the food the homestead owner offers as liberally as his means allow. This hospitality shown between family members and even between complete strangers expresses the unspoken bond of reciprocity on which their lives depend. With the increase in population, and those behind pressing on those in front, the time came to open up unoccupied land; so their fields were ever moving outwards and southwards.

The migration was a slow process, the groups at the forefront moving without a sense of the pressure of humanity thrusting up behind them, for more land always lay ahead and the land they vacated was always allowed to lie fallow for several years before new occupants moved in. But their general environment remained much the same and so did not promote the need for social and technological change. The red African soil, each grain covered with an insoluble pellicle of iron, generally brought forth enough food to keep the porridge pot full and, best of all, the cattle thrived on the grasses and the kraals were filled with the aroma of sleek and gleaming bodies.

Yet while the ratio of population to the carrying capacity of the land accounts for the rate at which people moved across the face of Africa, it was water that determined their route.

Africa is generally a dry continent, where only the equatorial zone receives a copious amount of rain. The particular bleached brilliance of the Afri-

can sky is a characteristic which derives essentially from the relatively low moisture content in the atmosphere in the interior of this massive continent. The splendour of sunsets over areas such as the Zambezi are also accounted for by the general aridity of the air coupled with the dull, red dust of the Kalahari sand hanging heavy in the sky as a veil through which the sun's dying rays are refracted and reflected.

In southern Africa, the summer winds, heavy with moisture from the Indian Ocean, blow westwards across the continent. At first, as they rise up the steep and narrow scarp towards the top of the plateau, they drench the land. But as they travel further, from east to west, so the rainfall decreases until along the west coast itself desert conditions prevail. Over the area which centres on approximately the Zambezi the equatorial system also influences the rains, but capriciously; they are often late in coming and then disappointingly brief.

Thus the Bantu-speaking migration reflects the fact that in broad terms the eastern parts of the subcontinent are more generously watered than the west. In Zimbabwe, for instance, the Eastern Highlands are liberally blessed with rain but in the west of the country the harsh scrub and ungainly baobab imbue the landscape with the hard and stoic evidence of recurrent drought. Adequate rainfall is, of course, vital to the farmer, but in many of the regions where it is plentiful, the land productive, and tree cover correspondingly thick, the tsetse fly, bearing the deadly trypanosome that causes *nagana* and sleeping sickness, is natural custodian of much of the best land. It kept the migrating people to the drier grasslands, and is endemic wherever in southern Africa rain exceeds 1 000 millimetres a year and there is shade, heat and humidity. It is a total deterrent to the migrating cattle man.

The general trend in the Bantu-speaking migration was south, but the distribution of its people on the subcontinent reveals the splintering of groups along the way. In Zambia, there are more than 70 distinct 'tribes', evidence that this region was a major crossroad for people moving south. Those who crossed the subcontinent, skirted the areas infested with tsetse and some settled in the Barotse flood plains over which the Zambezi spreads when in flood; and others – avoiding the fly country close to the Okavango Delta – came to

the northern reaches of Namibia and to the Atlantic Ocean beyond about 400 years ago.

Namibia is critically dry. The currents along her treacherous shore are chilled in the icy seas of the far south, and the cool sea winds bestow no rain: only the heavy sea mist that rolls in over the narrow coastal margin brings moisture to this region of grand and mystic silences, great serried dunes interspersed with pale calcrete plains. In the lonely spaces of this the Namib Desert, a unique endemic fauna and flora have evolved, peculiarly adapted to winning moisture from the regular sea mists and sustenance from the minute organic particles from time to time borne into the Namib by dry inland winds.

But to the cattle herders who reached these parts the miraculous wildlife of the Namib was irrelevant. They were interested primarily in grass and water, and the desert and the coast imposed a limit to their further expansion west. Some spread northwards into Angola; the Owambo settled on the broad plains beside the Cunene River, and the Herero looked southwards to find a home. Here, for the first time, they encountered competition from an unrelated group of herders, the Nama who had struggled over the thirstlands along the west coast, urging their cattle on in search of a place where they could prosper.

The Nama belong to a group known as the Hottentots (or Khoi), racially akin to the Bushman (or San). The main distinction between Khoi and San is cultural: the San were hunters of the wild animals of southern Africa's veld and gatherers of the wild plants; the Khoi also depended for much of their food on their intimate knowledge of the environment, but in addition kept cattle.

The Hottentot as a cultural entity is no more, killed off by diseases brought by foreigners to Africa and against which he had no immunity. Smallpox and measles decimated whole communities. The rest intermarried and were culturally absorbed by the newcomers, both black and white – or lost their lives defending their rights to the land.

All along the coast, however, from Namibia through to the Indian Ocean shore, archaeologists have uncovered numerous kitchen middens which reveal the *strandloper* (beachcomber) existence some of them practised. The huge mounds of refuse, including oyster and mussel shells, are testimony to the sustenance they gained from the sea. In Namibia there is reason to believe that even until quite recently the Nama resorted to the natural produce of the seashore when conditions inland became particularly severe.

The Khoi/San were the original inhabitants of the subcontinent – indeed there is increasing support for the theory that they evolved here. They are small and slightly built, and the marked accumulation of fat on the women's buttocks is considered sexually attractive. Their honey-coloured complexions, slanted eyes with pronounced epicanthic folds, and distinctive sparsely tufted hair seem to suggest a racial group completely separate from the other peoples of Africa. However, there is strong evidence based on somatic research that the Khoi/San and the black man come from the same gene pool.

We can only surmise the reasons for the separation between the southern and northern populations which led to their evolution into two racially distinct groups. Those of the north evolved into the negroid people with physical characteristics particularly adapted to tropical conditions such as heavily pigmented skin to screen harmful ultraviolet light, but the diminutive hunter-gatherers of the south have remained closer to the prototype from which both came.

The competition between herder and herder along the western reaches of the subcontinent has been a significant feature of Namibian history. The Herero and the Nama could finally go no further: each had to satisfy its territorial ambitions on the land between the deserts – the Namib on the coast and the Kalahari thirstlands further inland.

The conflict intensified with the arrival of additional peoples on Namibian soil – the more sophisticated Hottentot tribes who followed in the late 17th century from the Cape of Good Hope, bringing with them firearms which changed the balance of power in the encounters between Herero and Nama. Over the years, slightly more than a million people have settled in this area, including the whites who finally asserted dominance over the land and took for themselves great stretches of territory where they could herd their cattle and karakul sheep.

The discovery of Namibia's mineral wealth has increased the complexity of the age-old rivalries. There are diamonds here of unsurpassed quality, washed down to the sea by the great Orange River from the distant hinterland, uranium to power the nuclear reactors of the future, and minerals discovered but as yet untouched. Off southern Africa's west coast lies yet another valuable resource in this protein-hungry world: great shoals of fish such as pilchards and anchovy. Heedless plunder year after year has jeopardised the future of these fishing grounds, but with careful management and control they could still ensure a sustained yield.

In the face of such riches, the competition is becoming fiercer as each group tries to wrest power for itself and win the spoils. But the quest for power goes beyond the immediate protagonists. Behind the scenes foreign powers juggle for influence and try to tip the scales in favour of the group they guess most likely to prevail. In much of southern Africa where independence is either newly won as in Angola, or still disputed such as in Namibia, the jockeying of outsiders is a dangerously complicating factor. The flood of weapons channelled to the various factions makes negotiation less likely and unnecessary bloodshed more certain.

A century ago Nama and Herero could face one another in noisy skirmish and settle their differences with relatively small loss of life, but today the conflict has taken on a new and bloodier dimension.

On the eastern flank of the subcontinent the mainstream of the Bantu-speaking migration had pressed still further southwards and found the Bushman and the Hottentot already in residence. The Bushman had always known this land to be his own and roamed free and wide. Even the arrival 4 000 years ago of the Hottentots with their cattle, had done little to disturb his age-old freedom. But conflict inevitably arose with the arrival of the physically larger black man whose cattle took over their hunting grounds and whose iron-tipped spears and arrows gave him the advantage in fierce encounters. And when the Bushman discovered that domesticated cattle made far easier targets than the wary antelope of the veld, tolerance on the part of the black man gave way to anger.

He found these depredations intolerable, but the Bushman in turn saw his own survival threatened when the newcomers began to take things he himself cherished. Sweetness is a rare luxury in the

African veld and the Bushmen love wild honey, sharing the comb, the honey and the fat white larvae from the nest among the band as a special, much-desired treat. The black man, too, savours the dark fragrant honey and to the fury of the Bushmen plundered the nests he found.

But the subcontinent is vast and, especially in the eastern parts, sufficiently generous to accommodate them all: Bantu-speakers, Bushmen and the Hottentots living in the winter-rainfall regions at the far south. Although the grasslands give way here to tough-leaved shrubs which are not ideal pasture, the Hottentots by their skills at gathering wild foods had adapted to the environment.

But when the black man finally reached the area of the Sundays River beyond which lay the Cape *fynbos* (literally 'fine bush'), it was as if an invisible barrier blocked his way, for to him this was a hostile world. Not only was it poor cattle country, but more importantly, the millet and maize that had sustained him throughout his passage from northern lands did not flourish here. The advance guard explored the land ahead, but the people did not cross to settle; their technology was not geared to cope with the exigencies imposed by this foreign landscape. The migration had reached its natural limit. Yet the population pressure that had impelled it all the way south did not relax and the migration was now forced to turn back upon itself.

No written record exists to document the subsequent developments leading to the rise of Shaka and the Zulu in the early 1800s. The Zulu had earlier crossed the Drakensberg – the great mountainous spine dividing the western coastal fringe from the high and ancient plateau of the interior – and settled on the land along the coast of the Indian Ocean.

Several years of drought may have exacerbated a situation in which, through natural increase, the population had begun to run short of fresh land on which to live as cultivators and herders in the traditional way.

Impelled by land hunger and inspired by the leadership and military genius of Shaka, the Zulu set about plundering their neighbours. Armed with double-bladed assegais, superbly disciplined and motivated, the Zulu military machine conquered one group after another.

The Zulu first crushed all opposition as far north as the Limpopo, and the *difaqane* or 'forced migrations' ensued. Those who would not submit to Shaka's imperial ambitions had to flee, and refugees scattered far and wide, even reaching present-day Tanzania. Mzilikazi escaped with his followers to Zimbabwe where he founded the Ndebele nation, in the process thrusting aside others not directly affected by the Zulu. Like a stone tossed into a tranquil pool, the repercussions of these conflict-filled years radiated outwards in all directions, with permanent results on all the Bantu-speaking peoples.

In 12 years Shaka completely rearranged the distribution and allegiances of the black peoples of southern Africa. In 1828 he was assassinated, but for nearly 50 years more the Zulu maintained their dominance. Their final defeat at the hands of the British avenged the death of 1 600 men lost to the Zulu *impi* (battalions) at the Battle of Isandhlwana in 1879.

But a new force had entered the southern African arena. More than 300 years ago the Dutch arrived at the Cape of Good Hope. They were not the first foreigners from overseas to assert their presence on the subcontinent, for as early as the 10th century Arabs and Persians had set up trading relationships with people on the coast.

The gold of the Monomotapas in today's Zimbabwe was brought by Swahili middlemen to the traders at ports such as Sofala on what is now the coast of Mozambique. And, after the Portuguese became actively involved in the East Coast trade at the end of the 15th century, there was a constant outflow of ivory, gold and slaves. However, the Eastern visitors did not come to settle permanently and the Portuguese were satisfied to keep their dealings to the coast – although their demands, particularly for slaves, created havoc among people deep in the hinterland.

At the Zimbabwe ruins, the magnificent stone metropolis built by the Rozwi at the height of their influence in the gold trade, there are fragments of porcelain from the Far East. But it is doubtful whether any foreigner penetrated their empire and gazed at Zimbabwe when it was still a living city.

Unlike the Arabs and Portuguese, the Dutch who set up the tiny revictualling station in the curve of the bay below Table Mountain at the far south of Africa, had come to stay. Initially they simply provided food and water for passing ships. At heart, however, they were men of the soil, imbued with a pioneering spirit and a singular independence which soon asserted itself.

The need to escape the long arm of their government that kept so firm a grasp on its small, distant colony, became a priority among them. But even more important was the growing shortage of land in the immediate environs of the settlement. For the men whose herds were their livelihood, there was but one alternative: to seek fresh pastures in the interior. So inspired by the dream of finding land in which they would be free, they struck out beyond the mountains that ringed the tiny Cape settlement. In painfully slow ox-drawn wagons they wandered north-east, skirting the dry and frightening expanses of the Great and Little Karoos, looking for a home of their own.

Essentially they were farmers and herdsmen and as their path carried them ever closer to the land already long-occupied by the blacks, conflict became inevitable. When the whites who moved along the eastern margins reached the end of the *fynbos* they looked across to the *suurveld* with its literally 'sour' grasses. But for those who later managed to reach the land north of the Karoo, a far more rewarding vista awaited them; this was sweet grass country with streams of clear, pure water – and the black man already in residence.

This was the home of the Xhosa people, who were just beginning to return and settle down after years of death and disarray at the hands of Shaka. At first black and white pastoralist lived in uneasy peace side by side, but soon pressure on the land began to mount, arousing the spirit of angry competition over resources that remains a potent force today.

In the later history of South Africa, the distribution of resources – particularly land – along racial lines became entrenched and today the black cultivator is confined to a mere 13 per cent of the total.

Millions of blacks still live on this land, struggling to feed themselves. Their traditional method of shifting cultivation is impossible now that land is so severely limited and numbers are so great; indeed the pressure is such that it is not even possible to leave fields fallow to recover some of their fertility. Year after year they have planted the same earth, and with every harvest the yield has diminished until it is no longer worth working and is given over to cattle and goats.

Another little-recognised cause for concern in these rural areas – and in much of the continent as a whole as well – is the desperate shortage of firewood. The African peasant cannot afford to use paraffin to cook his food once he has cut down every tree within walking distance of his home, and he must now burn the cattle dung, depriving the land of yet another means of regaining its fertility.

The ravages follow an all too familiar progression: the soil is exhausted, the tree cover gone, and the forces of erosion go unchecked, turning the landscape in many of the areas set aside for blacks in South Africa into a wasteland striated with deep *dongas.*

The soaring birth rate compounds the predicament for while productivity of the land dwindles steadily, the need for food becomes more and more insistent. On the very land where the Zulu some 270 years ago felt the need for more territory to sustain themselves, some three million Zulu scratch and struggle to survive. Shaka would not recognise his former kingdom today, much of it is eroded down to bedrock and only the illegal fields of marijuana provide some income that keeps many from total starvation.

So the point has indeed been reached throughout southern Africa where any reallocation of more land currently being farmed on an intensive large scale does not solve the problem: these agribusinesses are feeding the subcontinent at large and to revert them to small-scale farming would be counter-productive. Only by teaching African farmers new methods can the current situation be reversed – or at least halted. And only by bringing down the birth rate will there be sufficient breathing space to make the changes.

It is useless to suggest that the peasant farmer should undertake capital-intensive, technologically sophisticated farming methods to make good the shortfall in productivity. He cannot afford the cost of fertilizer and pesticide, of high-yield hybrid seeds and the mechanization such methods entail. Instead a fresh appraisal is urgently required. For instance, the indigenous but often overlooked crops such as millet and sorghum may help to make drought-prone areas productive.

In many of these areas, the objective is not simply productivity but sustainability. For imported technology is not necessarily either suitable or desirable. The most productive farming areas in the world such as the American wheat-belt are also those that consume vast inputs of energy – not so much in human terms as in non-renewable resources. Africa cannot look to a future where these energy sources will be both sufficiently plentiful and sufficiently cheap to promise long-term rewards.

Agronomists and scientists must look to the African environment itself to establish the systems best suited to her and which will find easy acceptance amongst her rural populations. As researcher Paul Richards says: 'The least that can be said is that an idea borrowed from the people, developed by the agronomist, and returned to the people again is much more likely to be adopted than something totally alien to the culture.' The peasant farmers can no longer devote their energies to growing a single cash crop – disastrous market fluctuations in the past have left them unable to recover their investment both in effort and in money and simultaneously with too few reserves to carry them when things go wrong.

Meanwhile throughout southern Africa an alternative is to quit the land and seek a new life in the towns. But even South Africa with its broad-based economy cannot absorb all the influx, so the breadwinner often has to leave his wife and children to do their best in the village while he looks for a job in town. Without industrial skills, he frequently finds himself unemployed, without money to pay for accommodation, and joins the squatters on the outskirts of towns and cities. Lusaka, Bulawayo, Maputo, Cape Town – in all the urban centres the squatters are in residence, living under conditions that breed disease, engender despair, undermine health and destroy the dignity of the individual in his pursuit of a decent wage and a future for his children.

The poor agricultural land and a general lack of water are offset to some extent in southern Africa by immense mineral wealth. Coal and iron, copper and gold, chrome and vanadium, uranium and cobalt are but some of the riches with which nature has endowed the region.

Zambia's copper provides her main source of foreign exchange; Angola exports oil, and iron ore that is among the highest grade in the world. Huge deposits of low grade coal in South Africa are being transformed into oil, and the finest gem emeralds in the world have been discovered in Zambia. Namibia has diamonds and uranium, Botswana diamonds and coal, Zimbabwe chromium and high grade asbestos; and South Africa has a treasure trove of minerals from the gold which has for so long sustained her economic growth, to iron ore and vanadium.

Given these immense reserves of non-renewable resources, development throughout southern Africa has taken a similar pattern: the majority live on the land, eking out a living which barely keeps them at subsistence level, while the export of raw materials – minerals in particular – is the mainstay of the economy which, only in South Africa is diversified to any extent, although Zimbabwe and Zambia are industrialised to some degree.

The population has continued to grow at an unprecedented rate and gradually the children of today are being given some opportunity to acquire skills, and yet the economies have failed to develop the industries which will provide them with employment and circulate the national wealth. In too many instances the industrialisation that takes place is capital intensive in the western mould. In Africa today unemployment has risen to such levels and the unemployed create such socially and politically explosive situations that there can neither be stability nor growth unless every attempt is made to provide adequate work.

Several important considerations exist as to the form such developments might take. In Africa there has hitherto been a tendency in planning to prefer the grandiose to the simply practical scheme, to choose what will benefit the favoured few and neglect the many. For instance, one superbly equipped hospital may provide excellent care for those privileged to use it, but for the majority in the outlying villages and on the outskirts of towns basic clinics staffed by paramedics must surely have priority.

A similar principle applies in the manufacturing sector which tends to produce luxuries which few can afford while neglecting products suited to African markets and prevailing tastes. In countries with generally poor roads and a low gross national product there can be little justification for constructing plants to manufacture sedan cars when jeeps and trucks are needed and where all the man in the street can afford is a bicycle.

But the problem is more than one of deciding

how best to use resources – human as well as land, water and non-renewable ones. It goes beyond educating a child in abstract knowledge. The greatest problem ahead in Africa today as she gropes towards finding her own identity born out of an amalgam of the past and the present, her own cultures and environments, is that of values. The present and future generations must begin to bridge the gap between reality and expectation, for therein lie the answers to such urgent questions as population growth – and a better future for all.

For the foreign industrialist and entrepreneur, Africa is most attractive. Her mineral resources and raw materials seem to beg exploitation by a world which – particularly in the most highly industrialised countries – is already close to exhausting its own. Africa's current unemployment and underemployment situation also makes her labour sadly cheap and eminently exploitable.

And yet the temptation to take all now has pitfalls – not only for the African governments to whom foreign exchange is a vital means of sustaining their current populations, but also to the rest of the world. The global predicament is so real and so imminent that whether we like it or not, the race in which profit and growth are the ultimate goals is approaching the finishing line: beyond lies a sombre reality of a materially impoverished world. Therefore Africa should take care not to squander thoughtlessly her great potential and reserves.

**180** An African tableau of elephant, dust and a hot, orange-tinted sky.

**181** On the 16th November 1855 the great missionary-explorer David Livingstone was taken by canoe down the Zambesi River to see 'the smoke that thunders'. Nothing his guides had told him could have prepared him for the sight he saw. From a vantage point on a tiny island, he witnessed one of the greatest natural wonders on this earth: the broad, smoothly-flowing Zambesi dropping sheer over the lip of a falls 1 370 metres wide into a mist-filled chasm 108 metres deep.

There are higher falls in the world – and broader ones too – but none has the grandeur of the Victoria Falls or demonstrates so vividly the power of water.

The Falls are indeed a masterpiece of erosion cut by the Zambesi along faults in the black basalt that occurs along this part of its course. Through countless aeons they have reached their present site, and the zig-zag of narrow deep gorges below them etch their progress for some 100 kilometres as they retreated upriver, each gorge marking an earlier falls no less impressive than those of today. And still the river is at work, cutting into a weakness it has found along the lip, seeking a new fall line further upstream.

Others were to follow Livingstone. On the banks of the Zambesi, some 10 kilometres above the Falls, is a small cemetery shadowed by overgrowth, and all but forgotten. The inscriptions on the riverside graves reveal the fate of the little pioneer settlement; it had been abandoned after malaria had killed many of its women, its children and its men in their prime.

Malaria is still the greatest killer in Africa, yet it was but one of several tropical diseases against which over thousands of years the peoples of Africa had no real defence.

**182** On an anthill-studded plain, *Hyphaene* palms stand tall against a cloudswept sky. Every part of this graceful plant is used by the people in whose areas it grows: they make a sweet intoxicating wine from the sap and weave strong baskets and mats from the fronds.

**183-186** In magnificent costumes of painted bark and woven natural fibre, Mkishi dancers enact traditional set pieces. Among the Luvale people of the Zambesi flood plain each of these masks and its rôle is known, such as

Mongole (the hyaena) threatening and evil, and Nalindele the wayward girl. As the drums beat, the stories unfold, instilling in dramatic fashion the values of Luvale society, particularly among the boys who are about to be ceremonially initiated as men.

The highlight of the performance comes when one of the characters shimmies six metres up to the top of two slender poles. The spectators watch entranced by his supple acrobatics on the thong suspended between the tips.

**187, 188, 189** Talons outstretched for the strike, a fish eagle makes a shallow stoop over the Zambesi (187). Seconds later, with several mighty wingbeats it pulled clear of the surface (188), a great fish in its grasp (189). This is skilled hunting, depending for success on practice, power and precision.

214

*Previous page* (190): Lichen-blotched boulders of the Matopos seem to have been piled up by some giant hand. The largest population of black eagles in the world live here, preying on the hyraxes that scuttle about the boulders.

**191, 192** Few places in Africa have evoked more extravagant speculation than the Zimbabwe ruins, but archaeologists have proved beyond doubt that they were built by ancestors of the Shona people who still live in this part of southern Africa.

Late in the 11th century the Rozwi, a well-organized group of Shona, took control of the Zimbabwe hills which had long had mystic significance for the local people. There, among the granite boulders, they began to develop their kingdom on wealth from trade between the Swahili states on the East coast and the gold producers of the tsetse-infested lowlands. Within its elegantly proportioned and meticulously executed granite walls, the centre grew and flourished, and the Rozwi enjoyed the special pleasures of the very rich and very powerful.

On the evidence of such success the question must be asked: Why did Zimbabwe fall? The answer is no new phenomenon but chilling in its broader implications, for in the 15th century this vigorous metropolis began to feel the revenge of an environment heedlessly abused – the soil impoverished through over-use, the salt supplies exhausted, the wood needed to keep the cooking fires burning now well beyond reach, and the cattle had devoured every wisp of grass in the area. Zimbabwe could no longer sustain the Rozwi ambitions and lifestyle; it stands today as silent witness to the folly of ruthless over-exploitation.

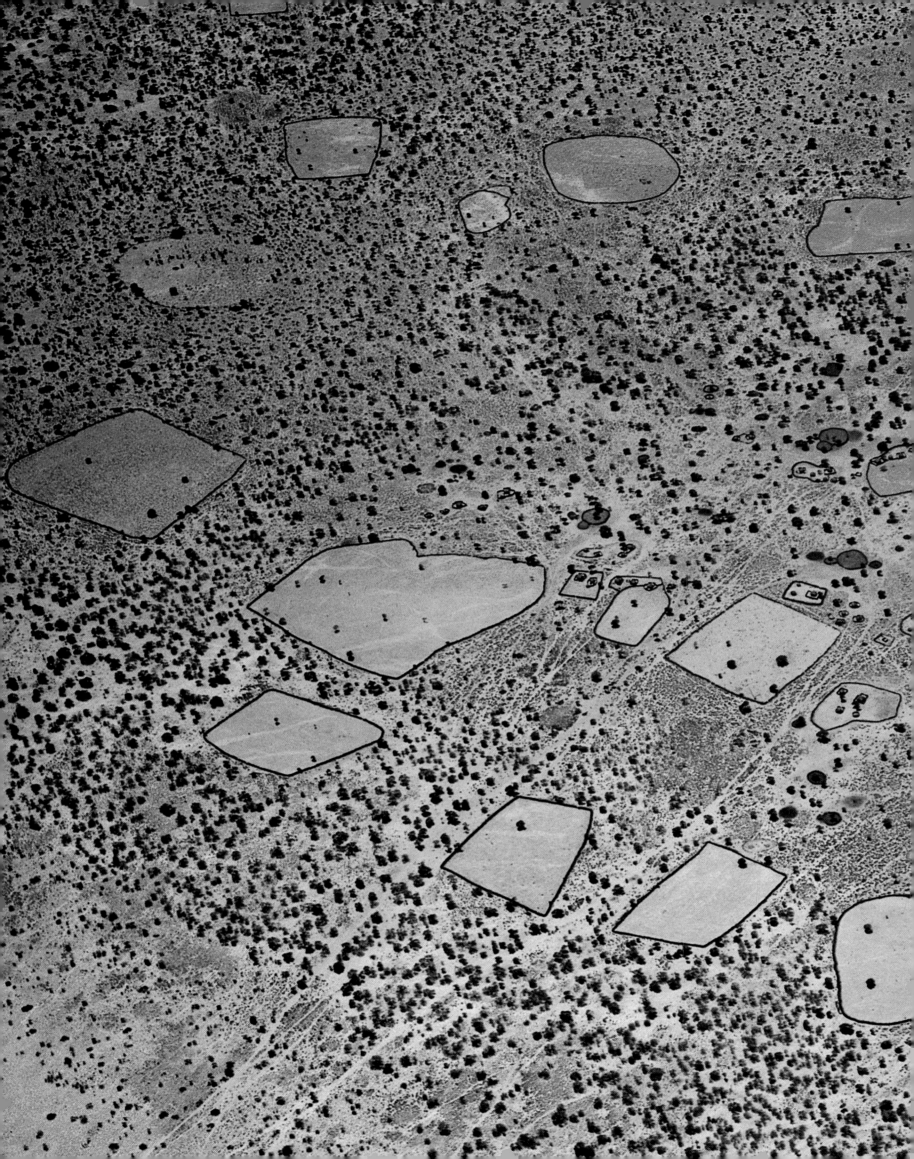

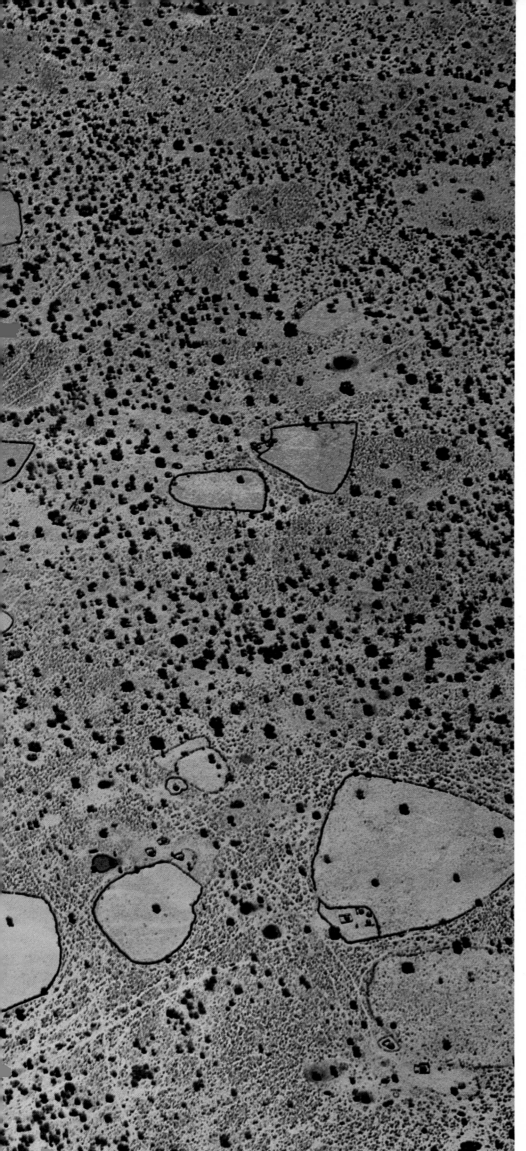

**193** On bleak Kalahari sands, thorn fences enclose barren cattle kraals. The herds have eaten up every bit of green within the enclosures where they are kept safe at night; except on the sites of old abandoned kraals where accumulated manure has encouraged a somewhat richer growth that shows up as darker patches from the air, the surrounding land is scarcely more luxuriant.

Infertile and widespread, the Kalahari is the largest unbroken mantle of sand in the world, stretching over almost a third of southern Africa and in places 100 metres deep.

*Following page* (194): Botswana is essentially a semi-arid country, yet in its midst is a vast wilderness of water 16 000 square kilometres in extent – the Okavango Delta. In a vain bid to reach the faraway Indian Ocean the Okavango River spills eastward to founder and die beneath the Kalahari sands. But before it does so, it fans into a maze of secret waterways filled with papyrus and strange waterplants that trail in its gentle flow.

Up until now the tsetse fly has been the natural guardian of the Okavango Delta for it brings sleeping sickness to man and deadly *nagana* – scourge to cattle. But a major assault on the fly has begun with sprays and pesticides and soon the Okavango will be more open to development.

These swamps mean many things to many people in this thirsty land and there are dreams and plans aplenty – pipelines taking water to distant coal and diamond mines; irrigation canals to make the Kalahari bloom; schemes to create new pastures once the water is drained away.

Many interests could be served and many voices heard but perhaps the most vital and eloquent are those of the conservationists urging wise and careful use. Inland deltas are complex and delicate areas easily destroyed. Like the tropical forests, these swamps are not as productive as they seem for the nutrients of the system are caught up in the existing natural cycles. Nothing is in excess and only the most careful and intelligent exploitation will ensure that the entire ecosystem of the Delta is not irreparably destroyed.

**195** Hambukushu women guide their dugout canoe to fishing grounds among the tall papyrus of the Okavango. This is one of Africa's last Edens; a place where hippo snort in the crystal waters and elephant crash unannounced through reedy sedges; where the last few river Bushmen still follow their secret ways and the equally shy sitatunga antelope feeds on aquatic pastures.

**196** Here some women set their reed fishing baskets side by side while others further upstream herd the fish towards the open mouths of the trap.

**197** A four-metre female crocodile stares malevolently at intruders to her nesting site. Despite restrictions, crocodile hunters have shot out many of the really big specimens and they sell the hides to make wallets and handbags and modish skin shoes, for here, in the Okavango, the outside world has begun its plunder.

**198** With arrogant disdain, a cheetah glares at the disturber of his post-prandial nap.

**199** The Kalahari is not a true desert but a thirstland where only creatures adapted to its unforgiving nature can survive. One of the most splendid is the oryx, a large scimitar-horned antelope peculiarly adapted to a life without water. By selecting the most succulent food-plants and feeding in the cool of the night, it takes advantage of moisture drawn up into the plants after the wilting heat of day.

Heat, as much as lack of water, is critical here and the straggly branches of the few trees offer but little shelter. For the oryx there is no relief. Patient and immobile, the oryx tolerates the intense sun, its large dun-coloured body absorbing the heat to the point where the temperature of its blood could permanently damage its brain. But its nose is specially adapted to meet this problem and blood destined for the brain first circulates through a cooling network of fine blood-vessels in the nostrils.

*Following page* (200): No two giraffe have exactly the same spots, but they all share the same long neck, developed for browsing among the tree tops. Slow and gentle, they delicately pluck leaves from between the thorns with their pointed mobile lips, and only when disturbed break into the elegant lope that carries them so smoothly across the plains.

198  199

**201** A lifetime in the Kalahari has weathered this Bushman woman's face, deepening her pale golden complexion to nut-brown, etching on it lines of humour and care.

Fewer than a thousand Bushmen still cling to a life as hunter-gatherers in the Kalahari, but it is possible that as a race they have never been more numerous for there are many, many thousand who have deserted these ancient ways.

Physically they are distinctive and unique. Their honey-coloured skin, high cheekbones and slanted eyes led many to believe that they were of Mongolian extraction. Genetic research has proved however the black man and the Bushman come from the same basic stock, and it is likely that the Bushman in Africa is closer to the prototype.

**202** The day before, the men had killed a giraffe, and today there is laughter and contentment in this tiny Bushman encampment deep in the Kalahari. The meat that could not be eaten at once has been cut into strips and hung (right background) on a pole to dry for leaner times.

But what of their children's tomorrow? Even now the last of the Bushmen as hunter-gatherers are being irrevocably drawn into the vortex of other cultures and in the process are losing their own.

201
202

**203** In the shadowed cleft of a secret watering-place, a Bushman hunter pauses to refill his water container.

**206** Ostrich strut below the smooth flanks of dry hills. For thousands of years the Bushman has known and used the eggs of this great bird. The contents – equal to two dozen hen's eggs – are made into an omelette baked in a coal-lined depression, and by taboo savoured only by the young and elderly. Undamaged egg shells are sometimes used to store water beneath the Kalahari sand, and in emergency the Bushman depend on these hidden caches. The damaged ones are broken into small pieces and worked into fine white discs which are then strung into necklaces.

**207** Snakes do not pose the hazard suggested by the western concept of Africa as a place of savage beasts and venomous reptiles. Most snakes are unaggressive and retiring by nature – given the option they would rather slither away than provoke attack from a larger animal. This sand snake eats lizards and is entirely harmless.

**208** Taller than a man and well over 100 kilograms in weight, the ostrich occurs widely throughout Africa. It was often represented in Egyptian hieroglyphs and its way of life was described in the Book of Job.

**209** Night falls quickly over most of Africa. Here the sun seems to hover for a moment, silhouetting the uncouth bulk of a baobab.

This tree, so typical of Africa's hot, dry, low regions, appears in the myth of many of Africa's peoples. The Bushmen say that when the Creator made the world he threw the baobab out of his garden and it landed with its head buried and its ungainly roots up in the air.

The black people of southern Africa have also come to revere these ancient giants, although they are not found in the well-watered lakes region of Central Africa from which they originally came. Collectively known as the Bantu-speaking peoples, they dispersed east and south of their earlier home more than two thousand years ago, probably because population pressure drove them to seek new pastures elsewhere for their cattle, and fresh soil to till.

Often spoken of as the 'great Bantu-speaking migration', this movement of black peoples southward was nevertheless slow and uncoordinated. As cattle herders they sought the sweet grasses of the savannahs as well as ample water. Furthermore, they had to avoid the regions where the tsetse fly was master for they dared not risk their wealth in cattle to the dreaded infection of *nagana* carried in its bite. But they were not simply pastoralists. Around their villages they burnt back the bush and planted sorghum and millet, beans and gourds. The women tended the vegetable gardens and worked the fields. In time, the population in any one place would build up, the productivity of the immediate vicinity would decline, and the people would move on. Following their herds, they moved into vacant land and this generally lay to the south.

By the beginning of the 12th century the Bantu-speaking peoples had come as far south as the Kei River in what is now South Africa and had populated the central and eastern regions of the subcontinent, wherever there was water. However, some crossed to the western coast, moving through what is now Zambia to the Zambesi River and from there westward by way of the Okavango Delta.

**210** A Himba woman, anointed with a mixture of butter and ochre and the allure of her beauty enhanced by the fragrance of desert myrrh. On her head she wears the tufted goatskin headdress of marriage, for the Himba who today live in the semi-desert areas just inland of the northern Namibian coast have clung to the old ways that are part of the Bantu-speaking tradition.

**211, 212** Caught up in the excitement of the night and encouraged by handclapping and urgent singing of the women, a Himba man (212) and woman (211) dance.

**213, 214, 215** In their dress the Himba express their love of ornament and their preoccupation with cattle. One young man wears the horns of a steenbok about his neck (213) while another, slightly older, proudly displays the four ears of heifers killed by his father and presented to him when he was initiated to manhood (214). Most prized among the women are the large cone shells which they wear suspended between the breasts. This woman's other necklaces are of twisted copper wire and slivers of mother-of-pearl (215).

**216** A Himba wife, milking one of her husband's cattle, uses a long stick to nudge the calf away from the udder.

The Himba, like the Masai, are bound by their culture to pastoralism even though their territory can no longer sustain this way of life. Mobility and plentiful land are essential to the traditional cattle herder, yet the Himba are now restricted to a certain, limited share of Namibia. However, because the size of a man's herd proclaims his status, the Himba cattle population has continued to grow irrespective of the land restrictions, turning their territory into an overgrazed wasteland.

Flexibility has always been one of the keys to human survival, but the Himba of today have entered a cultural cul-de-sac. Their cattle are in poor condition, their environment is in decay and their only alternative would be to change the very modes and values by which they have preserved their identity as a people.

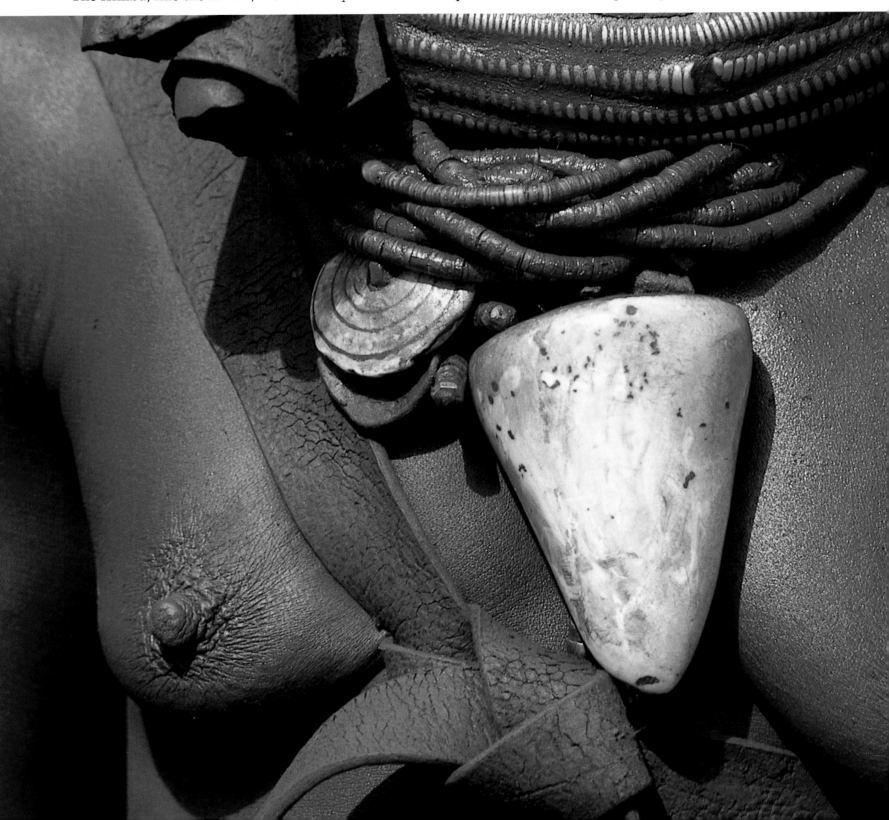

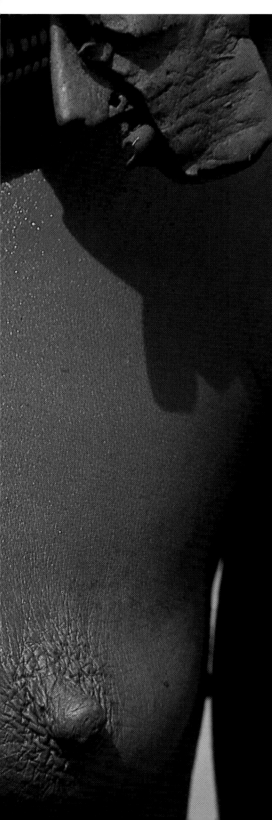

**217** In the midst of the Namib Desert is the Kuiseb River, indicated here by a trail of hardy plants. But the Kuiseb's riverbed is not always dry; intermittently — sometimes not for several years — it comes down in an angry torrent which reams out the accumulation of sand along its length and effectively halts the slow northward march of the southern dunelands (at right) from the grey monotony of the northern gravel plains (at left).

The Namib has been a desert from prehistoric times, and it has many faces. But most fascinating is the 300 kilometre-long dune sea south of the Kuiseb. Here the wind wails and moans as it ceaselessly shifts the sand, piling it this way and that.

What sets these desert dunes apart from those of the Atacama, the Baja, the Arabian — indeed from all the deserts of the world — is their surprising diversity of creatures all uniquely adapted to the numerous and singular habitats they contain. This apparently barren dunescape is the home of strange beetles and spiders and weird nocturnal reptiles, bright red scarabs, snakes and scorpions, web-footed lizards and the timid golden mole. Their survival depends on the cold sea mist that rolls in on one day in five and blankets the desert for up to 50 kilometres inland. To make use of this moisture, certain of the animals, by amazing behavioural adaptations only now being understood, 'drink' from the air.

On cold misty mornings, for instance, a black beetle the size of a thumbnail comes to the surface and struggles to the summit of a dune. Here it stands, its hind legs and body elevated into the damp air. Gradually, the moisture begins to condense on its body, forming droplets which dribble down the beetle's back to its mouth. By mid-morning when the mist begins to lift, the beetle is again buried deep in the sand to avoid the broiling desert sun; but later in the afternoon it resurfaces to forage for minute scraps of organic matter blown into the desert from more hospitable areas to the east. This beetle is just one of several creatures now known to draw liquid directly from the mist and to feed on the windblown detritus: the many other Namib creatures that cannot do so must in turn survive by feeding off those that can.

Since the combination of dunes, fog and dry land winds is in itself not unique to the Namib it is strange that similar creatures and plants have not evolved elsewhere in deserts where these three factors occur. The reason for its rich endemic flora and fauna therefore must be explained in a different context: that of its isolation and its age. For millennia the Namib has been a desert; and as such its perpetual dryness made it all but inaccessible to creatures from outside, providing a stable changeless world in which its specialised fauna and flora evolved.

218

**218** Fleshy-leaf succulents flower on the pale calcrete plains of the northern Namib.

**219** Stealthily hunting over the desert dunes at night, a palmatogecko consumes its hapless prey.

**220** Trees and grass beside towering Namib dunes at Sossusvlei.

*Following Page* (221): Herero women in their splendid national costume adapted from the dress worn by the wives of missionaries a century ago, gather for their annual pilgrimage to the graves of three great chiefs.

219   220

**224** To eat and not be eaten is a basic law of survival in the natural world. Here a rhombic night adder makes a meal of a red toad which was paralysed by the snake's venom.

**225** A herd of hippo snort and blow in a bend of the Levubu River. When darkness falls, they will leave the water to feed, their broad lips helping to crop the river-bank grasses.

The hippo has several features wonderfully suited to its amphibious lifestyle: its ponderous torso is hairless, and its nostrils placed on top of its snout can be closed when the creature submerges – sometimes for as long as five minutes at a time.

**226** The materials which sustain the creatures of the plains are caught up in a perpetual cycle in which death plays a natural part. The male lion pictured here, gnawing on a buffalo, is filling a predator niche in the ecosystem. Either through his excreta or on his eventual death, many of the nutrients which the buffalo obtained from the grasses will return to the earth.

There is no waste in nature's systems and once the lion has had his fill, the scavengers and minute decomposing organisms complete the job he began. Gradually, they break down the remaining tissue and bone into the original chemical components which then re-enter the life cycle through the roots of plants.

**227** Baby chacma baboons play under the watchful supervision of an adult.

*Following page* (228): A steam-driven train races through the snow-dusted foothills of the Drakensberg (Dragon Mountains) on its way to the east coast.

226  227

253

**234** Magnificent in the leopard skin denoting his high rank, a Zulu noble attends the Shembe festival.

In the early 1800s the Zulu were forged by their military genius, Shaka, from several loosely related tribal groups into a fighting machine such as Africa had never before known. Those peoples who resisted the Zulu yoke were either crushed or forced to flee from his superbly trained *impis* (battalions). The actual circumstances attending Shaka's meteoric career and the subsequent *difaqane* or 'forced migrations' of many of southern Africa's peoples are known in historical terms, but the environmental determinants for this aggression can only be presumed. However, at the time the Zulu began to flex their muscle, the great Bantu-speaking migration had already reached the limit of its southward thrust and this must have had a significant bearing on the events that followed. The barrier to their movement was as effective as a rampart wall: beyond the Sundays River they found a type of vegetation unsuitable as pasture, and further on a winter rainfall climate in which their maize, sorghum and millet did not thrive. To the Xhosa who spearheaded the migration, the land south and west held little promise; they had thus come to an ecological barrier beyond which some explored but did not settle.

But the population pressures continued, without more land available to absorb the growth. Territory had become a potentially limited resource and for Shaka and his followers the territorial imperative must have been an important motivating force. It has been suggested that several years of drought further aggravated the situation, creating the hunger and uncertainty which make war a means of survival.

In just over a decade Shaka changed the face of southern Africa. Refugees from his military campaigns streamed in all directions, bringing chaos even to those not directly affected by his imperialism.

Brave and highly disciplined, the Zulu army was to continue its military supremacy until the close of the 19th century. Then, after Britain suffered a humiliating defeat and lost 1 600 men at the Battle of Isandhlwana, the Zulu finally tasted defeat. But the memory of their former dominance of much of southern Africa is not forgotten – nor have the Zulu lost the proud identity they won with the assegai.

**235** A young Zulu woman does her laundry in a river.

**236** At night this Zulu woman rests her head on a special neckrest so as to protect her spectacular hairstyle, created by stretching the ochred strands of hair over a light wooden frame.

**237** A Zulu man in ceremonial dress.

**238** Teenage girls show off their colourful bangles, bead necklaces and the ear discs set into pierced lobes, so rarely seen today.

**239** Among the Zulu a fat woman is much appreciated and these young beauties at a special courtship dance will not lack for suitors.

**242** In the beams of their lamps some 2 000 metres below ground, a machine operator and his 'spanner man' drill holes for explosives in a gold-bearing reef in one of the seven goldfields of the Witwatersrand.

**243** Like the claw of some monstrous bird, a cactus grab drops excavated rock into a 'bucket' more than three metres in height. The 14 tons of rock are then hoisted to the surface.

**244** Beyond an eroded mine dump, Johannesburg expands both outward and up. Gold was discovered here less than a century ago and its effect on the economy of the country as a whole has been both dramatic and sustained.

In search of this precious metal, almost a quarter of a million men go underground each day. The main body of this workforce is migrant labour from the rural areas and neighbouring states and after their contracts expire they

**242**

**243  244**

usually return to their homes for they invariably leave their women and children behind when they come to *Egoli* – 'the city of gold'.

South Africa has experienced similar trends of urban migration seen elsewhere in Africa, but with some differences. Gold has provided the means and impetus for a diversified economy which has in turn provided benefits such as a relatively high employment rate. But the potential advantages for the majority of workers are offset by restrictive government policies which frustrate individual ambition.

In the already swollen – and still growing – townships on the outskirts of Johannesburg there is a continuing sense of bitterness and discontent. Since industrial development forged ahead in South Africa, the black worker has contributed significantly to the productivity of the country: today he is demanding his share of the national wealth.

**245** Xhosa huts cling tenaciously to hillsides scarred by erosion and virtually denuded of plants. Such desolate scenes are becoming increasingly common in the rural areas of southern Africa and are the inevitable result of too many people working the land.

When the Xhosa reached the southern limit of their southward movement, they settled in this area, now known as the Transkei, and used the land in traditional manner. Their villages were set on the better-drained hillsides, leaving the valley floors for cultivation. Their herds grazed pastures allocated by local chiefs – and distributed with a proper eye for conservation. Similarly, land was allocated among the people for the staple cereals and for the women's vegetable gardens. It was a system shared by most of the Bantu-speaking peoples and it had served them well in their long migration down Africa.

On the land set aside for farming, the women burnt the natural vegetation to make fields and then planted their crops. Since most of Africa's soils are poor, after two or three years they would produce less and less, and the old fields would be abandoned and new ones cleared. It might take many years before the particular patch of earth would be cultivated again, by which time it had recovered its fertility.

For this system to succeed there has to be ample land, and among the Bantu-speaking people this had always been so. Furthermore, this system made maximum use of resources with less manual labour than that required by intensive farming. But these circumstances have now changed. Millions must be fed off 13% of South Africa's land and, as this picture shows, under these conditions the peasant farmer's traditional methods no longer work. Not only have his herds cropped every vestige of grass from the land and rain washed the topsoil from his overworked fields, but to keep the cooking fires burning he has cut down every tree and bush, removing the last natural defence against erosion.

**246** Local grasses being woven into sleeping mats by an old woman at the Umngazi River mouth.

**247** In their ochred blankets, Xhosa women carry water to their homesteads from a nearby spring. Such dress is not truly traditional, for blankets were a Western introduction, and before the European came to Africa, Xhosa women wore clothing made of animal skins much as the Himba of Namibia still do today.

246
247

269

*Previous page* (253): Clouds promise long-awaited rain to the parched Great Karoo.

When the European at the Cape of Good Hope first looked beyond the immediate ring of mountains to the far interior, he found a barrier to his northward movement as hostile as the *fynbos* vegetation and climate had been to the southward movement of the Xhosa long before. This barrier was the Great Karoo – a vast table-land where water is extremely scarce yet in whose rocks lie fossils that tell of a time when it was the basin of an immense prehistoric lake.

**254** A whitewashed labourer's cottage surrounded by autumnal vines reflects the influence of the Dutch who colonised the Cape of Good Hope more than 300 years ago. And from the first tiny revictualling station created to serve Europe's trading interests in the East Indies, the white settlement of South Africa took foothold.

Essentially the white man at the southern tip of Africa was a tiller of the soil and herder of cattle. But he was also fiercely independent and soon looked to the African hinterland to escape the controls Europe maintained at the Cape. Above all he sought an African home for himself and his children. His first priority in this search was water; next was pasture. Driven by these needs, he skirted the Great Karoo and moved north-east until he reached the Kei River. There he gazed across to the sweeping grasslands which he had hoped to find. But, as competition for pasture grew so there was dispute between pastoralists both black and white.

Much of the later history of South Africa has echoed this early conflict over resources – particularly land. Even now the issue remains in essence the same: how are South Africa's resources to be shared and who will have the power to enforce the sharing.

*Following page* (255): Sir Francis Drake's 'fairest Cape in all the world', seen from the air. The African mainland lies to the left and the Cape Peninsula is seen trailing off to Cape Point in the distance.

254